The Bully and Me

Helen Carmichael Porter

The Bully and Me

Stories that break the cycle of torment

INCLUDES AUDIO CD

Northstone

Editor: Michael Schwartzentruber

Design: Verena Velten and Margaret Kyle

Cover artwork: Verena Velten

Proofreader: Dianne Greenslade

Northstone is an imprint of Wood Lake Books, Inc. Wood Lake Books acknowledges the financial support of the Government of Canada, through the Book Publishing Industry Development Program (BPIDP) for its publishing activities.

Wood Lake Books, Inc. is an employee-owned company, committed to caring for the environment and all creation. Wood Lake Books, Inc. recycles, reuses, and encourages readers to do the same. Resources are printed on recycled paper and more environmentally friendly groundwood papers (newsprint), whenever possible. A percentage of all profit is donated to charitable organizations.

Library and Archives Canada Cataloguing in Publication

Porter, Helen Carmichael

  The bully and me: stories that break the cycle of torment /

Helen Carmichael Porter.

Accompanied by a CD.

Includes bibliographical references.

ISBN 1-896836-79-8

  1. Bullying. 2. Bullying – Prevention. I. Title.

BF637.B85P67 2006   302.3'4   C2006-900006-9

Published by Northstone

an imprint of WOOD LAKE BOOKS, INC.

9590 Jim Bailey Road, Kelowna, BC, Canada, V4V 1R2

250.766.2778

www.northstone.com

Printing 10 9 8 7 6 5 4 3 2 1

Printed in Canada by

Houghton Boston Printers, Saskatchewan

Dedication

For the students who inspired the writing of this book.

Contents

Acknowledgments

I would like to acknowledge the support and assistance of the following people: my husband Gary Hophan, Rob Clutton (composer/musician-CD), Gordon Church, Rilla Clarke, Phillip Hophan, Jean Martin (composer/musician-CD), Pina Marchese, Prologue to the Performing Arts, Dr. Ron Ruskin, (the late) Dr. Peter Thomson, Rosemary Smith, Janet Stickney, Mike Schwartzentruber, Dr. Patricia White and all the parents, students, principals, teachers, and others who have told me their victim/bully stories.

Introduction

My Bully and Me

This book of bully and victim stories comes out of my own lifelong struggle with the bully within myself, which has always been there, whispering in my ear that I am "not good enough," "not capable of doing well," not "cutting the mustard." This bully is a twisted little imp, with pointed ears and wings and long claws. He has a terrible grin from ear to ear and, if you look at him closely, he resembles a gargoyle on a Gothic cathedral.

I coped with this bully in several ways. At an early age, I became a victim who was a pleaser, a chameleon, guessing what others would like me to be and then becoming that. I gave in quickly and adeptly, to make peace if friends or workers wanted something I had, or if they didn't want to do something I wanted to do. As an adult, I let my husband plan all our holidays and I enjoyed them, because it made him happy. I was a sincere flatterer, appeasing other people's own insecurities and self-doubt.

At the same time, I also became a *rebel* who countered the bully by stealing money from the penny mission box; telling little lies about who ate the whole layer of Christmas chocolates; and narrating scary ghost stories, which made me a popular if weird hit with kids of all ages. I was also able to tell stories that entertained adults and challenged the status quo: self-deprecating but humorous tales, with cunning portraits of bullies.

I was born with a fascination for hearing people's stories and a sensitivity that made people willing to share them with me. At ten, I was garnering tales from all the neighbors, but was forbidden by my parents to ever repeat or write them. "That would be wrong, that would be stealing." By the time I was 13, I buried my creative self deep inside and let the writer rest.

I never had trouble attracting and keeping friends, as I was most flexible, but also retained a wicked sense of humor. This combination won me wonderful, lifelong friends, most of whom are pleasantly dominating and accomplished. Like all victims, though, I got my own in secret by complaining, whining, justifying, projecting, ranting, and rationalizing my pain to a few chosen intimates (my father, a sister, a friend, a niece, therapists).

Where did this bully come from? As the baby in a minister's family, there were a lot of hurdles to jump. I consistently tried to be as good as my siblings and frequently worried that I wasn't going to succeed as well as they did in reading, writing, swimming, acting, etc. As a minister's child, there were rules and expectations, particularly that I attempt to be good in all my thoughts and deeds, something I failed at from an early age since I found being good intensely boring. So this moral bully probably entrenched itself in me deep and well, at a young age.

At first, I rebelled against it by imagining instead of thinking; by acting on my own impulses, rather than other people's. The negative feedback I received, mostly from adults but from some children as well, fed the bully, which lashed back inside, telling me I was "bad," "selfish," "stupid,} and I'd "better conform, or else!" I listened and obeyed, but also became a secret rebel, identifying with the bad and exciting characters I met in literature, including fairy tales, animal stories, comics, novels, and the best one, the Bible. Here I met characters like Cain and Abel, Esau and Jacob, Joseph and his brothers, King Saul and King David, Absalom and David, Queen Jezebel, Samson and Delilah, Peter, Jesus and Judas, Saul/Paul. Somehow, the fact that these nefarious characters and their stories were in the Bible helped me to stand up to the moral bully, who terrorized me on an hourly basis, and to support my own rebel.

Then, just when I felt I had evaded it, the bully came whispering that I was a "little pagan," that my heart was turning black with the number of lies I was telling and the amount of fun I was having, and that one day I would roast in Hell.

As I write this, I realize that these wild notions were absorbed by osmosis from my parents, who had been raised as Presbyterians before they became members of the United Church. In particular, my mother's Calvinist attitudes were imparted through little moral sayings, such as "Every time you tell a lie, a little black mark is placed on your heart," and "If you keep sticking out your tongue, one day it won't come back into your mouth," and "If you keep acting that silly, your eyes will stay crossed for the rest of your life." The result was that I split in three: the bully, the victim, and the rebel who became a counter bully. I conformed in my behavior to these "bullying standards," but rebelled in my mind and in my creative activities, which I hid from adults.

The bully and victim and rebel parts wrangled through school at all levels, with some checkered success. At university, at last, I ended up taking degrees in subject areas *I* enjoyed and wanted to study (English and drama). Still, however, the bully wanted me to teach instead of becoming an artist, and I conformed. This wasn't painful because I enjoyed kids and saw the potential for a creative life as a high school teacher. I had a rebellious desire to free up the system and to help kids become more creative and passionate in their response to literature and drama. But after five great years, and juggling these three psychic parts, fierce anxiety and depression arose. After some therapy, I resigned and, supported by my rebel, went into the arts.

Of course, the bully packed up and followed me there, where it initially took over. I spent a year trying to write, but my efforts were sabotaged by the bully taunts, "You're no good!" "That's drivel!" "Why do you even bother?!" The beautiful art of storytelling seemed like a compromise I could make without a lot of inner censure, so I became a storyteller instead. I have stayed this course well for more than 20 years. I appeased the bully by telling literary, biblical, and folk stories in schools and churches; in other words, I was helping others.

It was when I rebelled and established a theater and started to write plays that the bully rose up with increased intensity before and after every project.

As I continued to rebel, writing more and more shows to stay the bully, I unconsciously became a victim again by getting parking tickets! I'd park my car in and around the streets of the theater, which were no parking zones, and the tickets mounted up. I was so wrapped up with the task of writing, producing, and performing that I didn't notice that the tickets were my way of paying for what I wanted to do. It was when I received $3000 in unpaid parking tickets one day that I made a reckoning with the bully at the bank! At that midlife juncture, I decided that I couldn't live with this kind of fractured life and, close to a breakdown, sought treatment in psychoanalysis. As I went to my first appointment, I had the uncanny feeling that I was at a desperate place, which only this treatment could resolve.

That was in 1996, when the first bully stories were hitting the media. That spring a high school principal from a small town, which had recently suffered two events of gossip that led to a physical gay-bashing, invited me to come and work with his Grade 12 drama students, to put on an assembly about bullying.

Wondering what I was getting into, I drove out to the town and met twenty 17-year-olds who thought it was a complete joke to be trading bully stories as a source for assembly skits later that day. I knew that a few of these students had been suspects in the gay-bashing incident and I was curious to see what they would say. At first, they denied they had any stories from their own lives. Then, a big guy admitted he thought bullying was "cool." After this, one by one, the students disclosed childhood memories about how gossip and bullying had altered their lives. As I watched their assembly skits in the afternoon, I realized how much I identified with their situations. Driving back to the city, and over the next two years, my own memories tumbled forth, bringing back incidents with family and friends that I had repressed.

I returned to teaching high school half time for five years and began to tour a show called *The Bully and Me* to public and high school audiences. I wrote the stories in this first show from my own memories of family and school incidents, and from the memories and stories of a few kids. I did workshops as well, and children of all ages told and wrote their bullying experiences. In e-mails and letters, they wrote to tell me what was happening. Of course, I also witnessed scenes of bullying in the high school classrooms where I taught. Wherever I toured my show, teachers, principals, and janitors told me stories of similar harrowing things they witnessed and dealt with in their daily work. In the face of all this, I had no doubt that great damage and suffering was occurring to kids all over the country.

The stories in this book are imagined from the stories of over 300 children, teens, and adults, as well as from my own memories. As I've performed these in hundreds of schools, I've experienced a number of deep satisfactions. One is telling the stories of both the victim *and* the bully. Another is having kids tell me how good it is to hear a story about finding a way out and an answer to the bully. Especially satisfying is having bullies say, as a Grade 9 girl exclaimed aloud to her friends after a show, "Omigod, I'm a bully and I never knew it before!"

After ten years of inner battling with the three parts of myself, I think I have made some personal peace with them all. I am integrating them as one conscious mind. The victim and rebel and bully are three parts of my mind. What I thought was against me was just a part of me that I had disowned. In other words, I have, as in my story about "Justin," found my own power. I don't get parking tickets (much); my friends do what *I* choose sometimes; I don't commit to do things that I don't want to do; my husband and I plan our holidays together; if I can't drive my child somewhere, I say so. It has been a long and hard battle and much blood has been let. The truce has come by finding compassion for the bully and understanding that part of myself, and by letting the rebel have a voice without becoming a victim (paying for it).

This compassion requires that I be vigilant on a daily basis with myself. I get lots of exercise in this regard and have forged an arrangement whereby the bully part of me assists the rebel and the victim, and *together* these parts of me write and perform and live.

I hope that these stories will help victims to feel supported and bullies to recognize themselves and the two together to communicate and find compassion for one another.

1
Crystal

"I just want to go somewhere where nobody knows me."

It all started on the bus home, in Grade 6, when I was hungry and ate a little bag of tortilla chips from my Halloween stash. I wasn't hogging them or nothing like that. I offered some to my friend Stephanie, who was sitting beside me. Then this bigmouth kid Josh and his buddies TJ and Christopher started pointing at me and shouting, "Hey, hey, lookit what Porky's eating! Doritas! That's why she's so big!"

All these kids started laughing, even Stephanie, so I kind of laughed, too, but he kept it up. "She eats at McDonald's."

I turned around and said, "I do not!"

TJ, Josh's friend, said, "He's just kidding, you know. Take it easy." They grinned at me and everyone laughed.

At school, Elizabeth and Nicole, two skinny girls, heard Josh calling me "Pork Chops" and they started giggling and repeating it.

"Hey," I said, "I don't like you calling me names." Elizabeth replied, "We were kidding around." And Nicole raised an eyebrow as if I was so dumb to take it seriously.

I asked Stephanie if she thought that I was big.

"What do you mean?"

We were waiting for the bus, "Well, like fat."

She made me turn around, then said, "You look okay to me."

"Do you think that my butt is too big?"

Her eyes narrowed. "*Weeelll,* maybe you could lose two pounds."

The bus pulled up and we climbed on. I wanted to get on before Josh did so he wouldn't center me out as I came down the aisle, which was one of his favorite tricks. He and his friends always picked on kids who were different, like this nerd, Fraser, who was a computer freak, was named "Geek"; and this big fat boy, Bernie, who couldn't run around the gym, was called "Tank"; and a boy named Jeremy, who was a bit of a loner, was nicknamed "Gaylord" and "Pussy" and worse. Jeremy would sit at the back of the bus staring out the window, his face pushed against the glass, pretending he didn't hear. Even though he was older, in Grade 7, he didn't fight them back. Sometimes when these kids were getting off the bus, Josh and his friends would come up behind then and grab their backpack so they couldn't get off the bus. "Hey, let me go, come on, eh, this is my stop." But they would hold on till the kid sometimes had to rip their backpack to get away. Nobody could stop them.

When Josh and TJ got on, I looked out the window like Jeremy did, so they wouldn't notice me, but Stephanie, who was sitting beside me, called out "Hi' to them and Josh started, "Oh, Pork Chops, what are you munching now? Oink! Oink!"

I knew he was trying to bug me, so I didn't even look at him. He and TJ kept up running insults all the way home until the bus driver stood up and said, "All right you guys, will you SHUT UP now!" After that, they were quiet.

When I got home, I ran upstairs and looked in the mirror. I thought that I had a nice long brown hair, clear skin, and thick, curly eyelashes. I knew that I was growing bigger in my body, but did my butt look bigger than the rest of me? My mom said that I was a growing girl, but maybe this was too big. As I looked at myself, I decided to go on a diet.

At first it was easy. I had heard that eating white food makes you fat. So I cut out white bread, rice, pasta, potatoes. I also began running stairs at school and at my house. Trouble was, I was weak and hungry by 4 p.m. When I got home, I ate a bowl of potato chips. Then I purged, made myself throw up, the way I'd seen another girl, Melanie, do in the school bathroom.

Every day, Josh and others continued to call me nicknames. I hated when someone called me "Burger" or "Pork Chops." Whenever I told them to cut it, they said, "Oh, it's just a joke." I walked differently now, sucking in my stomach and straightening my shoulders so that I looked taller and thinner.

In class, I stopped volunteering to help the teacher and didn't put up my hand, even when I knew the answer. I didn't run for the bus or in the schoolyard anymore so I wouldn't jiggle. I started hanging out more with Elizabeth and Nicole, even though they whispered to each other in front of me and sometimes called me "Pork Chops." When I told them I didn't like that name, Elizabeth smiled: "I think it's cute; I didn't mean anything."

My mom started to notice that I wasn't eating much at the table. She didn't believe in kids going on diets. One night she said, "Why aren't you eating your pasta? I made that for you."

"I don't like pasta anymore."

My dad said, "What? That's ridiculous! You've always loved pasta since you were one year old."

"I don't want it! I just like the meat sauce."

"I made it for you, Crystal. Are you on a diet?" My mom was looking me in the eye.

I didn't answer.

"You look the perfect weight for your bone size and height."

My sister Angelina, who's 15, said, "You're a bit young to be on a diet and you look fine. The girls in this family all have a big butt. Some guys like that, believe me!"

My dad added, "Girls need their calories just as much as boys do, so eat up for your strength."

"I just want to lose five or ten pounds, Dad."

"Why?"

"Oh... some kids on the bus said stuff..."

"What kind of stuff?" asked my mom.

"They called me names like...'Porky'...and...uh...'Lardbutt...'"

"What!?"

Angelina rolled her eyes. "That's kids. They say the meanest things just for the fun of it. Just ignore them."

"I've done that, and they still do it."

Dad added, "You have to fight back, Crystal, not go on a diet."

"I've told them off, too, but they say they're just joking. They pick on other kids too."

"Would you like us to phone or visit the school about this?"

"No! That makes it worse! Jeremy's dad called the principal and the kids have been meaner to Jeremy ever since, mostly behind his back."

Mom said, "Well, you need to see the doctor for a checkup, so maybe when you hear what he says about your weight you'll realize that you are the right size for your bones and not listen to these kids."

"Good idea!" My dad rose from the table. "You look just terrific, Crystal," he said, hugging me on his way upstairs.

After we'd seen the doctor, who said I was in the correct weight range for my age and height, my mom and I went shopping for some new jeans. We had dinner out and I ordered chicken fingers and fries with veggies. My mom smiled: "It makes me happy to see you glow. The next time anybody calls you a name, you tell them to stop, right now. Just tell them."

I wore my new jeans on Monday, and though Josh hooted, "Here comes Hippo," when I came down the aisle of the bus and some kids laughed, I pretended I didn't hear. Stephanie said, "I like them."

When we got to school, Elizabeth waved, "Hey, Crystal, we want to talk with you! Hurry!" She and Nicole were standing with their friends under the trees by the playground.

Elizabeth's face was pink with excitement. "Do you want to be in our MSN conversation group? We're only inviting our friends."

"Can Stephanie be in it, too?"

"Well, we've just chosen and well, all right, but that's it; we don't want too many, do we?" Elizabeth looked at Nicole who was wearing the same hoodie as Elizabeth, only in powder blue that matched her eyes. "We're just asking people who are our friends," Nicole added.

"Cool," I said.

I was excited that evening when there was an e-mail to the whole group from Elizabeth telling us we were "the most popular kids in

Grade 6" and who did we think was unpopular? Nicole answered with a list of names: "Tiffany, Lisa, Dougie, and Stephen."

Melanie added: "Tiffany and Stephen."

Even Stephanie added: "Lisa and Dougie."

Elizabeth wrote back, "y r they unpopulr?"

The others replied, "Lisa smells bad," "Stephen has ugly teeth," "Tiffany's a skank," "Dougie's a moron."

I waited to see what other topics they'd come up with before I'd write and every message after that was about "Jennifer's awful hair," or "Megan's stupid pants," or "Lee's dumb face." They wrote about which boy liked which girl and who didn't like who.

The chat group was controlled by Elizabeth and Nicole. If I wrote an opinion of someone different from them, they didn't reply. Or if I tried to change the topic to something else, they didn't pick up on it and no one continued with a topic introduced by someone else unless Elizabeth and Nicole were writing replies to the topic. Even though it was mean, I ran home to get on the computer to see what they were writing today and sometimes I wrote stuff about kids, too.

One night I received a message that had no sender: "Why don't you disappear, Fat Girl. Nobody likes you; you're so fat and ugly."

I stared at it. Who would write me something like that? I deleted the message and next day I watched and wondered who had sent it. The next night there was another one saying, "Hey Pig!! Why do you eat so much? Nobody thinks you're good looking."

I stared at the screen for about five minutes. I thought about telling my mom and I knew she'd visit the school and those kids would all find out. No. It was better to just pretend that I hadn't received them and maybe they'd stop.

I didn't tell the girls in my group as we all knew that only seriously unpopular kids like Jeremy got vicious e-mails. That's why his dad visited the school in the first place.

The next week, when I got on the bus, I noticed that Josh, Chris, TJ, and Stephanie were each looking at some paper and when I came down the aisle, they quickly put it away. I noticed that other kids had them too and were looking them over. "What's everybody reading?" I asked Stephanie.

She said, "You're not supposed to see."

"What is it?" She wouldn't answer. "What is it!?" I repeated.

Then she brought it out and handed it to me. It was a computer printout of a pig who was a girl, with hair like mine and wearing sneakers like mine. Underneath was written: "For Sale! A 200 pound pig for $1 a pound."

Someone had crossed out the $1 and put in $.50 and then crossed that out and put $.10.

I held this in my hands and felt my face get warm. I tore it up and handed it back to Stephanie.

"I don't know who did it," she said. "It was sent on the computer last night and TJ printed copies for kids."

"Why did they do this?"

She shrugged. "I dunno. I'd ignore it if I were you."

At school, I could tell that other kids were looking or had been looking at this paper by the way they looked at me and then away with a smile on their lips. I decided to tell the principal and went down to the office. The vice principal said that the principal was away so I told her and she asked to see the paper. I didn't have it. When she went looking for one no one had it. Every kid said they didn't have one. She visited every Grade 6 class and made an announcement that anyone who e-mailed kids negative messages would be suspended. When she spoke to our class, the kids stared straight ahead. No one offered to tell her anything. At lunch, Elizabeth said, "You know, I'm glad you reported it. No one should get e-mails like that, even if it's a joke."

"It's not a joke," I muttered, but said nothing more. I actually wondered if Elizabeth and Nicole might have done it, because I couldn't think of anyone else who would have done it. Also, Elizabeth's cyber name was "sugarbabe" and I saw that that was the name scratched out on the printout.

That night, when I went home, there was another e-mail. "Hey, Pig, everyone thinks that u r so a disaster, the way u walk, the way u dress. We'd spit on you, but we don't want to waste it on nothing!!"

I went downstairs and picked up my backpack and carried it up to my bed. I emptied it and began to throw stuff in: pj's, underwear, socks, sweater, jeans, ski vest, Walkman, fav DVDs, my diary, notebooks, extra runners. As I packed, I made a plan. I still had the money that my granny had sent me – $100 on my birthday. I was planning to buy some new sneakers, but now I knew that I would buy a one-way ticket to her town up north, where she and my aunt lived. My aunt was the vice principal of the public school there and would be happy to have me. How many times had I heard my granny say that she would love to have me live with her? I couldn't count. We were so close and it was the perfect answer to my problems. My mom and dad would never let me go, but I couldn't stand to spend the rest of the year at my school. I wrote a note to my parents.

Dear Mom and Dad:
I am leaving to go to Granny and Aunt Gillian's. I'm going to go to school up there. Don't worry about me. I'll call as soon as I get there. I love you very much,
Crystal

I left this note on my pillow the next morning, when I left for school. All day I went about my school and if people called me a nickname or my own name or nothing, it didn't matter a bit because I was thinking "I'm free, I'm free; I never have to go to this school again after this. I never have to see any of these jerks again." I ate lunch with Elizabeth and my friends, but they never guessed a thing. When I told Stephanie that I wouldn't be on the bus because I had an appointment, she said, "Okay, see you tomorrow."

I left the school and walked through the park behind the school to Wilkins Street, then to Smith, and then through the high school track and over to Main Street. It took me almost an hour, but the longer route kept me from seeing anyone from school. So far, so good. I knew from last summer when I went with my mom that the bus for the north stopped on Main Street for customers every day at 5:15. I had 15 minutes left. I sat down on the bench by the bus stop to wait. It was getting cold. I was glad that I'd worn my ski jacket. I watched the cars and trucks driving past, hurrying to get home. Across from me was a Texaco station, and beside that a medical building and a variety store. I wondered if I had enough time to run across and get a chocolate bar for the bus trip.

Suddenly, I heard, "Crystal! Is that you? Crystal!"

I looked around wildly. Who had called me? I looked in the cars and trucks passing, but I didn't see anyone. I looked across the street. "Over here, Crystal!"

There, on the corner across the street, I saw Emily, a girl from my class, one of smartest kids in the school. She'd won first prize at the science fair. What was I going to do? The bus would be here any minute and she'd see me getting on.

"What are you doing here?" I called.

"I was at the doctor's there and I'm waiting for my dad to pick me up," she called as she crossed at the lights and came up to me.

I thought about what I should tell her, so she wouldn't go back and tell anyone. She was short and had red hair and glasses. Kids called her "Four-eyes" and "Hobbit," but she was popular too. She actually never called anyone a name. She was also very independent. Kids respected her because she was confident, too. She was also an old friend of Elizabeth. They lived on the same street and had been in the same daycare.

"What are you doing here, sitting by yourself?" she asked.

"Waiting for the bus."

"Where are you going at this time of night?"

I looked at her gray eyes and wondered if I could trust her. "Can you keep a secret?" I asked.

"Of course," she said, and moved in to hear what I was going to say.

"I'm running away," I confided.

Her eyes widened. "Why?"

"I can't stand it at our school anymore. I'm going away."

"But why do you hate it? It's a good school, good teachers and everything."

"But kids don't tease you as much as they do me, Emily."

"What teasing?"

"You know, calling me 'Pork Chops' and stuff like that and saying I eat at McDonalds every day. And then the e-mails I received. I can't stand it."

Emily nodded. "Yea, it's gross the way some kids act. But you know, running away is just what they want. You shouldn't run away, you... Uh... why don't you let my dad drive you back home and then in the morning I'll meet you when your bus gets to school and we'll... uh, hang out... and if anyone calls you a name, we'll... uh, bop them on the nose together, we'll stop them."

"Why are you saying this?" It sounded crazy to me and I wondered if she meant it.

"Lookit, I think you're cool. I want to be friends with you and stand up to this kind of meanness."

"Why do you think I'm cool?"

She looked at me. "Well, you run away by yourself, you're waiting to take a bus at night somewhere, you've got some guts... Oh, there's my dad, come on, let's cross!... Daddy, Daddy, over here! Can we drive Crystal home?" she shouted across to a man in a van.

When Emily and her dad dropped me off, my parents were freaking. "Where were you? We were phoning and looking for you all over the neighborhood. We were just phoning the police to report you missing!" Their faces were pale and my mom's eyes were red.

"Bye, Emily!" I called. "See you tomorrow."

She and her dad drove off.

We came into the house and I told my parents what I had done. They hadn't found my note.

"Why would you run away?! You have everything a kid could want."

"I'm going to visit the school tomorrow and tell that principal that something has to change," my mom said.

"Mum, that won't help. Me and Emily have a plan."

"And what's your plan? You're just two young girls. How are you going to fight something like this?"

"We're going to hang out and if someone calls me or anyone a name, we're going to stop it."

"How?" my dad asked.

"Uh, we're going… to bop them on the nose. You know, stop them!"

"Well, I'll let you try this, but if nothing changes, we're going to step in and see the principal. This is serious."

I looked up at them. "Emily's dad thought we had a good plan. Give us a week."

The next day on the bus Josh and TJ made the "oinking" noises when I got on, but I ignored them. Just you wait, I thought. Stephanie had no idea what was going on and I didn't tell her.

At school, Emily was waiting for me when the bus rolled up and she had a huge grin on her face. "Come on, let's walk around the yard."

We walked and talked and laughed and Josh and Christopher called, "Oh, look at Porky and Shrimpy! I didn't know you were friends."

Emily marched right over and said, "What did you say, Josh?"

"Yeah," I said," What did you say?"

He flushed and said, "You heard me."

Emily said, "Did anyone ever tell you that it's dumb to call people names?"

"Aw, get real, I was kidding. Is that a crime?"

Some kids had gathered to watch and Josh turned redder. Christopher came up. "Whaz happenin'?"

"He thinks it's a joke to insult people about their body size and shape and he doesn't know why we're complaining."

"Yeah," I suddenly added, "he insults anyone who's different from him, as if he's so perfect-looking."

Other kids laughed and Josh looked angry. "What's with you girls? Are you lezzies or something? How come you're doing this?"

Emily spoke clearly. "I know that it's ignorant to call people names about things they can't do anything about, like the color of their skin, or their weight, or height, or wearing glasses, or parents, or anything. And we're not going to let you ruin our school by doing that."

"That's right!" I echoed. More kids had joined the crowd around us, asking, "What's going on?" "Wazzup?"

Emily said, "Whenever you pick on someone, we're going to speak out against it and maybe others will too."

I echoed her again. "Yes, we mean this."

All day we hung out at recess and ate lunch together and if we heard anyone call someone a stupid name, we spoke up: "What's your problem? Why do you have to put others down to make yourself look good?"

This went on for the next three days, our walking around, calling out if someone insulted another kid or picked on someone or spread rumors about them, and kids began to notice.

Jeremy said, "Thanks, you guys," and Tiffany and Lisa and Stephen and others asked if they could "help us."

Elizabeth and Nicole said we looked dumb, but we ignored them.

Mrs. Brown, a teacher on yard duty that week, told us, "You girls are something else. I didn't know about half of these problems. Good for you!" And she told the rest of the staff.

That's how the principal heard about what we were doing and called us in to tell him about it. After he heard about the e-mails and the name-calling and my running away, he asked us to write up a full report of what happened to me and Jeremy and Bernie and lots of others, and how Emily helped me. We took a couple of weeks to do this and my mom helped a bit with spelling and grammar. Then we gave it to the principal. My mom also sent a copy to the Board of Education. After they read our story, they started a Bully Program in every classroom! All the teachers had to read our story and then take some training. Our janitor made a Bully Box, a wooden box with a slit in the top, and this was placed in the office. Kids were told they could write their stories if they were being bullied and put them in this box and the principal would read them.

My parents were so proud of me and Emily. My mother said, "I have to take back what I said, that two girls couldn't do anything. You two are amazing."

Emily and I are now in Grade 8 and we're still best friends. Sometimes we hang out with Elizabeth and those kids, but we're also still busy with our own bully work. We want to make sure that what happened to me is history.

Commentary

Crystal is a typical Grade 6 girl who wants to fit in with the popular crowd. Others, sensing her need, take advantage of her size and shape. Though she tries to ignore it, it's impossible because her close friends are involved. When your best friend is calling you names, what do you do?

This is by far one of the most common stories I hear from kids, but that doesn't mean it doesn't wound them in a deep and lifelong way. The bullies in this story pick on kids' sexual identity, their weight, their addictions, and their differences – all at a vulnerable age. The result is a vicious underworld of gossip and taunting that shapes the social atmosphere of the public school.

Victims, unable to cope, become depressed, or turn to addictions and negative behaviors instead of reporting on the bullies and getting some action against them.

Crystal decides to run away and might have been successful had she not run into her classmate, Emily. Emily is the kind of rare student who *does* get attacked and bullied, but doesn't care. She identifies with her parents, no doubt, and practices that rarest kind of thought, common sense. She believes that what the kids are doing is wrong and she sets out to change it. She seems immune to the opinions of her peers, yet she knows how to communicate and be a good friend. She is a model for how kids could change things if they forgot about being popular and thought about helping kids who might be sidelined by the rivalry and competition in middle school and higher.

I advise kids who are being bullied to write about their experiences, even if they are afraid to show what they've written to anyone. At least they have a record of the day, the place, the persons involved, and what occurred. I notice that when they keep records, they start to feel indignant about what is happening and feel more confident to show their notebook to somebody in authority. Regardless of what they do with it, writing about their experience can be healing and empowering. "The pen is mightier than the sword" is true in more ways than one. By writing, kids release the rage and hurt, and feel more grounded in themselves.

Parents can learn much from this story, as can teachers. Kids can change things, if they feel empowered to do so. The enlightened educator and parent can create the right circumstances for that to happen.

Activities and questions for discussion

1. Make a list of times, places, and the people involved, when you were bullied as a child, teen, or adult. Describe what you did about it and how you felt.
2. Have you bullied someone or seen someone being bullied? What happened, how did you feel, and what did you do about it?
3. Does your Board of Education sponsor a conflict resolution program? How could you take this program and help others to put into classrooms?

2
Kyle

"I'm not a bully!"

Hey, at first I didn't know why the kids said I was a bully. I didn't mean to do nothing to no one. Maxwell's broken nose was an accident, totally.

It happened like this. He and I were horsing around outside the library after lunch. He pushed me and I pushed him back, both of us kidding, and ka-boom! The floor was still wet from winter boots, and he slipped and stumbled over his humongous feet and fell down the stairs. If he hadn't put his hand out to grab the banister, he wouldn't have smashed his nose so hard at the bottom and busted it. I ran down the stairs to help him, but he yelled, "Get away from me! You pushed me on purpose!"

"I did not, I did not!" I said, and then our teacher, Mr. Marshall, came down and helped him up.

Maxwell told Marshall, "He did it on purpose. He wants to hurt me."

I said, "That's a lie and you know it."

Marshall helped Maxwell down to the office and they had to drive him to the Emergency to get his nose set.

Well, I felt bad enough for him, as my buddy Ben will tell you, because he was with me and he knew I was fooling when I teased Maxwell, or anyone.

I always laughed when I teased him and his runty pal, Dylan. Oh, yeah, we called them "faggots" and "Dorfus" and "Goof," but he never said anything that it bothered him. And, like I wasn't the only one! Everyone made fun of this guy; he couldn't even run once around the backfield without heaving and just about throwing up. He's got no stamina or talent in sports, but that doesn't mean I hate him or nothing.

Yet he said that I did, and that he felt *persecuted* by me. Persecuted! At least that's what his parent said to the principal, Mr. Lang.

So, next thing you know, I was called down to the office and laid out on the carpet for ganging up on Maxwell. Lang showed me into his office and shut the door. It was kind of dark in his office, as the walls were wood-paneled. "Sit down please," he said.

"I didn't mean nothing bad with Maxwell, it was an accident... we were, uh, horsing around, and uh..."

Lang cleared his throat. "You have upset a number of students. Maxwell is just the latest. A parent called me yesterday saying that you're terrorizing students with your sarcasm and insults, and your taunting and name-calling. It seems that you're a menace."

I'm a menace... a menace? I couldn't believe what he was saying.

"You turn kids against other kids, and, as a result, the school isn't safe with you in it."

"Who are these kids that said this?"

"They're terrified of you so they won't speak to me; a parent did. He knows the effect you are having on the other students. He's heard them talking in his home."

"But I have lots of friends and everyone knows that I play around a lot; I'm just fooling with people."

"Well, you know that whenever there's an altercation at this school, you're usually in the middle of it and you always say that – 'I was just fooling.' I don't believe that, Kyle. I think you'd be better off if you were transferred to a tougher school that has tougher rules, teachers, students."

His mouth was a firm line, like a ruler, something I'd never noticed before.

"But I'm almost finished here; I graduate in June. My marks are good. And... and all my friends are here."

I stared at him disbelieving. He had to be kidding.

But he picked up some papers from his desk. "Five months is too long a time to risk having you in this school. These are the transfer papers for you. I'm calling your parents to come in and sign them. I've called this school and you can start next week."

The bell rang for change of classes, but we didn't move. I sat there, looking at the rug, my mind blown away by this. I said, "Why are you picking on *me*, though? There are other kids who do the same things. Ewen takes pictures of kids being beaten and e-mails them to other people!"

"I'm dealing with him as well, and others, but that's not your concern right now. Actually, several parents have complained that their children are afraid of you, that you play rough and people get hurt. One mother said that kids didn't want to be in the same classroom as you. I warned you last fall that I didn't want roughneck play on the school grounds. Yet you've kept it up, regardless of what I said."

Jeez, I thought, who are these wusses who are scared of me? I wondered what he was going to tell my parents. My heart pounded, my mouth dried up, my knees shook; I felt as if I was going to cry. I was thinking, this is happening because he thinks I'm a bully. But I'm not, I'm not, I'm not.

I said, "But... but I'm not a bully, sir, you have to believe me. I was just kidding around. I didn't mean nothing by calling Maxwell a fag; it was a joke and he knew that. I was kidding when I laughed at Brittney; I mean, I was just about fooling about her weight."

"What did you call her?"

"I called her a pig."

"That doesn't sound like a joke to me. That sounds pretty cruel."

"I like her, actually. I just meant she looks big."

"You see, Kyle, that's your main problem; you don't think that you're a bully. You don't take any responsibility for what you do to other kids. You say it was just a joke and walk away. Well, that won't cut it any longer around here."

"But I'm not a bully!"

Mr. Lang leaned forward across his desk. "You're bullying me now, raising your voice, telling me, the principal, that I don't know what I'm talking about."

"Oh, no, no, well, I didn't mean that. I, I... just know that I'm... not a... a bully."

"How do you know this so well? Do you have something to tell me?"

I looked up at him. "I live with a real bully!" My voice was barely audible.

Lang narrowed his eyes. "You *live* with a bully? What do you mean by that statement?"

I gulped. I mean, the last thing you want the school to know is your private stuff, like you don't want them to know your business, but I was desperate. I didn't want to transfer and I didn't want my parents to know.

"Do you promise not to tell anyone?"

"Just tell me why you are not a bully."

"Well, my brother Sydney? He hates me. He's five years older and he hates me. I don't think he ever wanted me to be born, at least that's what it feels like. I mean, my first memory is my brother knocking me on the head with the remote control because he didn't want to watch my cartoon on Saturday morning."

Lang was writing some notes on a pad of paper, but he interrupted, "You know that Sydney was a very solid student here a few years back. He was also one of our best hockey players. All the teachers... everyone liked him."

"I know, I know. My parents pushed him into hockey so he wouldn't be so aggressive at home. He's a good student, too, but he's always fooled adults so they don't see what he's really like. If I ever told my parents how much he picked on me, he'd get me, no kidding. He used to grab my arm and twist it up behind my head, or sit on my chest till it really hurt so I would do what he wanted. If I cried and told my parents, he'd always pretend that it was an accident or that I had asked for it by teasing him."

"Are you sure you're not exaggerating his picking on you?"

"NO! Do you want to know how he greeted me every morning

when I got up? He'd growl so my mom didn't hear, 'Get out of my way; I want to have a *good* day.' Or if I bumped into him or touched his stuff, he'd hiss, 'Don't *touch* me or my things! I don't want to get AIDS.' At the table, he'd refuse to look at me, or make faces when I spoke, circling his finger around his ear like I was mental. He liked to call me 'retard,' 'suck,' or 'peabrain'."

"What did your parents say when they heard him talk like this?" Lang asked.

"He was sneaky. He usually whispered it or said it when they weren't around. If they *did* hear it, he'd say, 'I'm sorry; I was just joking'."

"How did he take advantage of your age?"

"Since he was so smart and since he said I was so stupid, he was always correcting me, especially when we hung out together, like on our holidays, when we'd be playing board games or building forts, or something, and he'd continually say, 'You're copying my design,' or 'You cheated,' or 'You're really stupid, you know that?'

"When we were swimming at my grandmother's lake, he pushed me under after my uncle told my mother that I have 'a good strong stroke.' Sydney didn't like me looking good. He actually held my head under water after that and I had to struggle to get back up for air! He just laughed like it was nothing, but I couldn't get my breath for a minute or two.

"Then, another time, in the winter, we went tobogganing on the big hill near our house and he was supposed to be looking after me. He and his friend Sebastian let me go down once, and then they just kept going up and down with some friends they met up with, while I stood there freezing. Sydney didn't care. He just told me to 'stop whining,' like he didn't care if I froze. Sebastian made him take me down a few more times, because he felt sorry for me. But when I cried because my feet hurt, Sydney punched me. 'Oh come on, don't be such a wuss.' My feet were almost blue when I got home and my mom asked him what happened. He lied: 'Kyle didn't do his boots up right and he didn't want to move around, so his feet got cold.'

"I told mom he was lying and that he had ignored me, but he said *I* was lying. Later he twisted my arm so it really hurt. He said, 'That's for telling Mom lies about me, you little weasel.'

"He punished me a lot for telling on him. Once, when he babysat me, he locked me in the garage and left me there for half the evening while him and his friends played around on the street. When he let me out, he said I'd get it good, if I told my parents. I was so afraid of him, I never told."

"This kind of rivalry is fantastic," Lang said, and wrote some more notes on his pad.

"When I started school, Mr. Lang, it got much worse, because Sydney couldn't stand to see me do well. Like, I started to read well, and in Grade 1 I brought home a book called *The Happy Prince* that my teacher lent me to read to my mom. While I was reading it, Sydney came in from hockey practice and he interrupted. 'That's a kiddie version. That's not the real story.'

"My mom told him to be quiet. He got his coat off and listened some more and began clapping his hands in this loud way, making fun of me. 'Isn't that great?' my mom asked him.

'Yeah, he's a good reader,' he said, 'but it's a kiddie version.'

'He's only in Grade 1,' my mom reminded him.

"Later, he stopped me in the hall and said, 'You think you're so bright reading a fairy tale. I read *The Lord of the Rings* when I was in Grade 4; you'll never do that, you're too dumb.'

"I asked Mom if that was true and she said he read it in Grade 4 and 5.

'See,' I told him, 'you lied!'

"His face went purple and he clenched his fists and he said, 'Don't you ever touch my books or you die!'

'Oh, yeah? I'll read what I want to.'

'Not my stuff.'

"Like, my brother was so jealous of me, he couldn't stand to see me reading a book. He'd come by and say 'Oh, look at Kyle, he's READING, oooohh.' And if I told him, 'Shut up will you? I can read what I want,' he'd look at me and say, 'Don't you know when I'm kidding you, moron?'

"He made me so mad, because he wouldn't leave me alone and let me grow up, so I know that I began to pick on him and take his stuff sometimes just to bug him. Of course he'd flip out and then I'd say that I was just kidding."

"What did your parents say about all this teasing and fighting?" Mr. Lang asked.

"Nothing. They were used to it and Sydney lied to them. He always said that he was just playing with me. They didn't see what he really meant. But my uncle Rob did. He was a wrestling champion in high school and college and he started helping me, showing me some arm moves and leg holds, which I started using on Sydney. Boy, that surprised him, because I practiced a lot. Uncle Rob said, 'You just do a few of these and he won't pick on you any longer.' And he was right. Sydney was more careful about pushing me when we watched TV or horsed around anywhere."

"Did you use some of these moves on kids at school?"

"Oh, no, well, only if they bugged me, then I might. Like there was this wise guy in Grade 3, who beat up people smaller than him, and one day I flipped him with a leg hold and he never picked on me again."

"But it might have frightened other kids, that you were so good at wrestling."

"Maybe."

"Sydney was a good solid student. There isn't a teacher who would say he was a bully. This seems to be your opinion, Kyle. And I wonder how all this could make you act the way you do now, picking on weaker students as you seem to do. That's a bit of an excuse to me." He removed his glasses and looked at me closely. His eyes looked sad.

I was shaking. "It's all true! He's not what people think; he fools adults with his smile and manners. He fooled my granddad."

"What happened there?"

My eyes filled up with tears and I had to swallow this huge sob that suddenly came in my throat.

"Take your time," Mr. Lang said, and offered me the box of tissues on his desk. I blew my nose.

"About three years ago, my granddad on my dad's side, and his girlfriend, Lisa, came to visit for a week. Grandad said, 'Lisa and I are going to Florida for March break and we want to take one young man with us. He must know how to behave in hotels and restaurants, and he might want to visit Disney World. We'll stay near a lagoon that is full of snakes and crocodiles. It's in the Everglades. And we'll go fishing.'

"Both of us said, 'I'd love to go, Grandad. I'd behave the way you wanted.'

"Grandad said, 'Well, we'll be here with you for a week, so we'll see who the real gentleman is and he will go.'

"Lisa added, 'This trip will be so much fun.'

"Me and my brother were on our best behavior all week. We never fought once. We helped serve the table, asking Grandad and Lisa whether they wanted more rice, or meat, or wine? We each cleared the dishes and piled up the dishwasher and helped Dad in the kitchen.

"Grandad and Lisa played board games with us in the evening and we never squabbled over the rules or the action. They also took us out separately to places we chose, like to see a movie or go bowling and have pizza.

"Grandad told my mom and dad, 'These are well-behaved boys.'

"Mom laughed. 'Well, stick around a little longer. They're on their best behavior for you two.'

"Actually, Sydney was making faces at me big time behind Grandad's back, but Grandad never caught him doing it.

"At the end of the week, I came home early and was watching a show I sometimes watch after school when I'm tired. Suddenly, Sydney came in and threw off his coat and grabbed the remote. 'This sucks,' he said, 'I wanna watch *MuchMusic!*' and he changed it just like that without asking me.

'Hey!' I said. 'Turn it back.'

"He took the remote and smacked me on the side of head with it and stuck out his tongue. I grabbed the remote, but he wouldn't give it to me. He pushed me off. Then I grabbed his arm and twisted it hard and he cried, 'Owwww,' and his face went all white and he got up with his arm all limp and went upstairs to show my mom. I sat there and changed the channel and went on with my show, because I knew he was putting on an act.

"I heard him moaning and my mom putting cold towels on it or something, and then my granddad came downstairs and said, 'Hey, what happened?'

'Nothing,' I said.

'Nothing? Your brother's arm is practically hanging out of its socket and you say *Nothing?*'

'He changed my program.'

'What? You're telling me you twisted his arm because he changed your program?'

'He's lying. He came down here and pushed me around. He hit me with the remote like he always does and I grabbed his arm. I didn't hurt him. He's putting on an act.'

"Grandad said, 'Your brother is up there with a very sore arm, which he can't straighten out, and you don't seem to care…'

'He punched me and took the remote and cracked me on the head with it after he switched my show!'

'That's not what he says. He says he never touched you.'

'He's lying and I didn't touch him hard.'

"Grandad scratched his head and said, 'I never thought a grandson of mine would be a *bully*, but that's what you are, Kyle. Anyone who can twist their brother's arm because he changed their channel and then go on merrily watching their show without showing concern for what they did is a bully.'

"He went upstairs and I stayed downstairs watching TV.

"After supper, Mom told me that Grandad and Lisa were taking Sydney to Florida.

'Why?' I asked.

'I think because Sydney's older and it's a long time to be away.'

"I knew Mom was trying to protect me. Later that night I asked her, 'It's because I twisted Sydney's arm, isn't it?'

'He never actually said.'

"I knew Grandad had believed Sydney's story that I had picked on him for no reason. It was hard to say goodbye to Grandad, I felt so disappointed.

"Sydney smirked at me and whispered, 'Nah nah, you get to stay at home.' There was a gleam in his eyes, like he had won.

"I said, 'I never wanted to go in the first place. Who wants to be stuck in a car with old people all day?'

"Sydney said, 'You're a poor loser'."

Lang looked up. "Is that why you pick on other kids, and get kids to gang up against someone else?"

"I'm trying to show you that I live with a *real* bully," I said. "I guess I learned to stand up for myself because I had to do it so much with Sydney."

"Do your parents have any idea about the negative influence he's had on you?" asked Lang.

"I don't see how they could. Sydney can be pretty convincing."

"I can see that. But do *you* see that living with Sydney has made you a bully?"

"Maybe..."

"Good, well...," he stood up and stretched, "I want you to know that I think you are a strong kid to be able to tell me all this. Your story has made me rethink my decision to transfer you. I know a lot about bullying, because I was bullied by my older sister and my neighbor when I was a child, in some pretty mean incidents, and I know how it can affect you for the rest of your life. That's why I'm not putting up with it in our school.

"Now, even though you've been a victim at home, you've been a bully at school, Kyle, and I have to call your parents and tell them about this. They have to help you at home. I also want you to take a course here at school, with some of the other bullies, so we can do something about it now. You may go now."

He opened his door and ushered me out of the office.

I walked home in a daze, thinking Mr. Lang was bullied by someone too? It was impossible to imagine this big, tall, bald man being bullied.

I had no idea what happened, but my parents dropped by the school to see him after work, and when they came home that night they called me and Sydney to sit down for a talk. They told us, "Things have to change in our house. You two are brothers and you are not to tease or insult each other any longer. If we hear you fighting in any way with each other, we will withhold your spending money and other privileges, like driving the car and going out with friends."

They didn't say nothing about Mr. Lang or my being transferred, so I didn't mention it either.

The next day at school, Mr. Lang called me down and told me he was starting an anger management program he'd designed called "Red Light." There were four other kids who had to take it with me. Ewen and his friend William, and two girls, Erin and Rahal.

This meant that the five of us had to stay at school two days a week for a month, to watch some videos and answer questions in a notebook, and practice Lang's exercises. Lang said he based "Red Light" on this book call *Taming the Tiger*. It was written by some Eastern teacher called Thich Nhat Hanh, who teaches peace and stuff like that around the world.

First, we had to learn to recognize when we got angry. It's all physical – your heart and head race, your stomach clenches up, and you feel like hitting something. Then we had to stop and ask ourselves, who am I angry at? Usually, it's not the person you're attacking; it's someone you know well, in your family. For me, it was my brother; for Ewen, it was his dad, who's really nasty when he drinks; for William, it was his step-dad, who has a mean temper. Erin said she wasn't mad at anyone, but after a while she admitted it was sort of her mom; and Rahal said she hated her sister.

After that, we had to see how we aimed that anger at teachers or kids at school, kids like Maxwell and Brittney, who we think are weak and won't lash back. Then we had to learn how to visualize a red light, so that when we get mean or physical against someone, we stop and imagine a red light in our mind. A red light means STOP, so you do. Then you count to 20. By that time you have calmed down, and you can think about your anger. Where does it come from? Who am I really angry at? When you've answered those questions, you visualize a green light, and now you make a positive decision not to attack someone. Instead, you try to find a creative or peaceful solution.

At first it was really hard, but I kept it up and Mr. Lang said I was a fast learner, and had helped everyone else in the group by knowing and telling my story.

We all had to practice the "Red Light" program at school and at home. Whenever Sydney insulted me, I visualized a red light and counted to 20 and changed the subject, or left the room. It was hard, but I kept doing it day after day. He couldn't figure out what I was doing. After a while, he stopped. He seemed nervous around me and then the strangest thing happened. We started talking about sports and music and movies. We even watched some hockey games together. One night he said, "Hey, *The Matrix* is coming back to the theater and me and Sebastian were planning to go on Saturday. Do you want to come?"

The Matrix was his all-time favorite movie; he was always talking about it and now he wanted me to see it with them. I never imagined my brother and I would ever be hanging out, like friends.

In May, Mr. Lang asked us all to put on some skits about anger control in Assembly, and to train some younger students in Grade 6 and 7 so they could carry on the program the next year. We taught them everything we'd been learning and practicing since January.

Finally, it was Grade 8 graduation night. As I looked in the mirror before I left for the graduation dance, I checked out my new haircut, suit, and tie. Something seemed different. When I left the house to pick up my date, I knew what had changed. All my life I had been a victim, which had made me a bully. But now, I was neither. I was just me, a guy, 13 years old, called Kyle.

Commentary

Kyle is a bully who doesn't know himself as one until he is caught and made to face his acts against others. His anger and bitterness towards his brother has corroded his own heart and mind, and he feels no guilt for attacking kids at school. Mr. Lang provokes him into telling his story about being a victim at home. Usually a bully denies his or her vulnerability; only when Mr. Lang brings up the transfer to a tougher school does Kyle show his own pain. Mr. Lang has an unusual awareness of bullies and how they operate. His confidence in working with tough kids is shown by his own revelation to Kyle about being bullied as a child.

When a student can tell their story without fear and shame, their problems are greatly changed. Adults who know the power of storytelling can help bullies and victims to understand themselves by getting them to tell their stories.

While being a victim made Kyle a bully *to others*, some victims became bullies *to themselves* and knock themselves down with negative self-messages and paralyzing self-doubt. By telling their story, they too can come to understand their inner voices and discover where these come from. They too can be freed like Kyle and become themselves, unafraid to show their power to the world.

Educators and parents can help students enormously by listening to their stories and by telling their own. This can only occur when you are aware of your own past and are willing to mine it for your life stories.

Activities and questions for discussion

(Can be used with adults and youths.)

1. In pairs or in small groups, tell a story about a time when you were bullied and include all the details of who, where, what, and when. Next, tell a story about a time when you were the bully, incorporating the same details. After this, share a few of these stories with the whole group/class. End by discussing the thought patterns of victims and bullies.

2. Write a bully diary in which you describe recent incidents of bullying in your home, neighborhood, store, park, or school. What patterns do you notice in the behavior of bullies and victims? Is there anything you could do to change or stop these situations?

3. Think of someone who is currently a bully to you. How could you change the dynamics so that you no longer feel this way? What has stopped you from doing this before?

4. Look in newspapers for stories about bullies and victims (e.g., robberies, wars, etc.). Cut these out and bring them to class. In pairs, analyze the motivations of each person and develop strategies for how they could change their position in this scenario.

3
Mandhur

*"I don't know what I would do
if my parents found out…"*

When I was 11, I thought I had a perfect life. I was a straight-A student; all the teachers said the same things: "Mandhur is bright, dependable, a pleasure to teach." I was pretty. I'm not conceited, but I do have nice skin, a small nose, and a slender body. I was popular and had no trouble attracting boys.

My home was special too. "We're not like other immigrants," my father liked to boast after a big family dinner. "How long have we been in Canada? Four and a half years and look at what we have," he'd say, waving his hand in the air so that all eyes would take in our brand-new, four-story house, all landscaped with a separate apartment for my grandparents. "You kids are spoiled with your own entertainment area on the fourth floor," my mother added, "and with your 50-inch TV screen, sound system, and computer terminal, you are all set. You have everything… clothes, music, sports gear, games, whatever you need." My grandparents listened and shook their heads; they thought it was too much.

My brother and I nodded when they talked like this. We saw my dad drive off every day to work hard with my uncle in their import business and we wanted to make them happy. We knew, as my grandfather said many times, "He's doing it all for you kids." In return, my parents expected us to do our best and they trusted us to do so. But why wouldn't they? As their older child, I never did anything to disappoint or disobey them. I followed their rules.

My dad had many restrictions about boys and parties and sleepovers. He sometimes checked over my e-mails and, once, when my friend Samira had written some things about a boy who was cute, he screamed, "You will never like a boy that is not our choice! You and your friends know nothing. You are not part of this culture and you never will be. Remember, Mandhur, it's not *you* that I distrust; it's the world around you. You are my daughter and you do what I say. Do you understand?" He only approved of me going to school dances because they were chaperoned and held during the day. At these dances, I could only dance with girls and had to be home as soon as the dance was over at five o'clock.

It was at the Halloween dance in Grade 6 that I first noticed Rafe. He was tall and dark-haired, had huge eyes, and seemed more independent than the other boys. He was dancing with Grade 8 girls, nodding his head and keeping the beat with his hands and feet. He and his friend Sajinder hung out with older kids. They weren't like the boys in Grade 6, who were always shoving and punching each other, and danced like elephants. Watching him dance with these girls in the dim orange light of our gym, I decided that he was too old for me.

Later, I thought that he and his friends were crazy. On dress-down days, depending on the theme, they came in wigs and silly clothes like pajamas or long black trench coats, or dresses and crazy hats, and they went around the schoolyard singing pop songs in loud, hoarse voices. Then I heard gossip that they hung out with high school kids at the mall, and did drugs. When my girlfriend Tammy started going with Sajinder for a while, I thought she was really dumb.

But one October morning, in Grade 7, Rafe and I both came running into the schoolyard late. He had his backpack flung over a shoulder and his hair was wet, curling on his forehead. His shirt was half on over his T-shirt. He smelled like spice. He rushed up to the door, then saw me and stopped. A smile broke across his face. His brown eyes were so bright they took my breath away. I smiled, too, and then looked away. He grabbed the door and held it open for me to enter first. He gave me a quick once over, whistled, and turned away down the hall.

After that, I looked for him every day in the hallways, the cafeteria, the schoolyard, and thought of a hundred things to say to him. I was surprised by my own silliness. It was as if Cupid, the little god of love in the Roman myth we studied in Grade 6, had shot an arrow into me when Rafe opened the door! I couldn't stop talking about him with my friends.

My friend Samira advised, "Look, I've heard that he's strange. He hangs out with druggies, like Marcus and Sajinder." Tammy whispered, "He's got a girlfriend anyway. She goes to high school."

I decided that it was unwise to like him after hearing that, but it was no use. I couldn't walk past him without quivering. I played and replayed that morning meeting, when he held the door open, over and over in my mind like a repeating tape.

Still, he never spoke again to me other than to nod when we met. This was weird for me because other boys noticed me and tried to win my attention. I wondered if Cupid had shot an arrow into his heart as well as mine that morning. Maybe not. Yet it seemed that the more negative things that I heard about him, the more I liked him. Of course my parents didn't know anything about him, and when at dinner one night they said that I would marry one of their friends' children, I nodded my usual yes, as if that were my dream, too. If you knew my father, you'd understand why I did that. He would kill me if he thought that I would be attracted to a boy he didn't approve of.

I loved my father and I would do nothing to make him angry.

One day, out of the blue, everything changed. Rafe smiled at me in the hall and in the schoolyard. His friend Sajinder e-mailed Tammy that Rafe wanted me to be his girlfriend. And I had wondered if he liked me! The next day he came up to me at noon, as my friends were returning from the corner store. I couldn't believe it; his eyes were so bright and his dark hair now had blonde highlights... he looked so cool.

He said, "I think you are so good looking. I've been too shy to talk to you."

I blushed, "That's what you say to everyone."

"No, I mean it; you are gorgeous."

I didn't speak, and then he bent down close and murmured, "Hey, do you wanna chill with us?"

"Where?"

"Over at the mall, after school; that's where we go." He indicated his friends who were waiting for him, laughing and joking with each other.

I said, "I heard that you had a high school girlfriend."

"Yeah, but we broke up. I'm single again."

My heart was pounding hard. "Well, I can't go to the mall. I'm not allowed."

Rafe shook his head. "That's too bad. I suppose you're not allowed to have a boyfriend?"

"You're right. My father is strict."

I thought that would put him off, but it didn't. Every day he came over to hang out with me and talk about what I'd been doing.

"You live in Meadow Heights above the river," he said. "Those houses are so big."

I laughed. "Yeah, it's nice. Where do you live?"

"On the other side of the mall."

I couldn't imagine introducing him to my father – that wouldn't happen for a long time. We started to hang together at school, in the yard, and afterwards in the park behind the school. Everyone could see by his attention that he liked me. We were often with his friends, but it didn't bother me. They joked a lot and dressed well and had more money than most kids.

All the girls were talking about us, these good-looking Grade 8 girls who liked him. They gave me dirty looks and spread rumors that I was having sex with him, which made me laugh because their jealousy was so transparent.

Samira, who reported all these things to me, said, "He will trash you. You will be hurt by this boy." Tammy added, "I went with Sajinder for six months and he was poison, remember."

I knew that Sajinder had recently lied and dumped Tammy and that she was mad about it. As well, these girls were jealous of me because I was popular with boys and not afraid to be different. I waved at Samira, "Thanks for the warnings, but you don't really know him and his friends;

they are all very nice; you have to get to know them."

Rafe and I never even held hands at school. But when school got out, sometimes we went into the park behind the school and kissed and fooled around in the grass behind the bushes. His friends stood on guard. Like other girls did with their boyfriends, I was willing to do anything with him, except I wouldn't have sex. I told him that.

Samira and Tammy said, "You are taking such risks, girl."

I shrugged, "He's my boyfriend."

One day, a few weeks after we'd started going together, Rafe came up to me and said, "I need some money. Can you get me some?"

"How much?" I asked him.

"About $100."

"Are you crazy?" I spluttered.

"What's the matter? You're rich, I bet you get that for allowance!"

"But I don't have that."

"Well, you can get it, can't you? Don't your parents have money?"

"They'd never give it to me for a boy!"

"They wouldn't have to know. Couldn't you take it?"

My dad and mom keep a lot of cash in the house, thousands of dollars in a box. And they use it for household shopping. But they would notice if $100 went missing.

I looked up at Rafe. His dark eyes were not smiling, he looked desperate: "I need it."

I wanted to help him. "I can only get you $50."

"When?"

"Today, if I go home right after school."

"We'll wait here in the park for you."

When I got home, everyone was out except for my grandparents. The only sound was the ticking clock on the mantel. I tiptoed up to my parents' bedroom and found the money box in the top shelf of their closet. There was at least $2,000 in the box in mostly small bills, so I counted out $50. My heart was pounding and my hands trembling, as I placed the lid back on the box. I promised myself that I'd pay it back with my allowance.

As I came back downstairs, the door opened and my grandfather came in. "What are you doing home?" he asked.

"Oh, I forgot a book that was in my room," I said.

"Don't be late," he said and went into the kitchen. I left the house, shaking.

When I gave Rafe the money, he called to his friends, "Got it! Let's go." They took off without looking back, except for Rafe, who shouted, "I'll see you."

Watching them disappear over the hill to the mall, I felt weak, as if someone had hit me in the stomach. I didn't even hear Samira and Tammy till they were standing behind me, shouting, "Hey, are you deaf? We've been calling you across the park!"

Tammy laughed, "Girl, you've got it so bad, you don't see anyone but Rafe."

Samira said, "We never see you much anymore."

I nodded at them and smiled. "I haven't been avoiding you. It's just that we hang out after school. That's the only time that I can see him. The mall is off limits and that's where he hangs with his friends."

We started walking out of the park and I noticed them exchanging looks.

"What? What are you guys looking at me like that for?" I asked.

Samira pushed her hair back over her shoulders. "We don't want to make trouble, but…" She looked at Tammy for help.

Tammy spoke carefully: "Rafe is seeing another girl behind your back. He's meeting her at the mall."

"Who? Who!? Someone in Grade 8?"

"No, no, she's somebody's sister, a real skank, everybody uses her."

"I don't believe you. Rafe would tell me."

"You're fooling yourself, girl!" Samira cried. "You're being stupid!"

I looked at my friends' sorrowful faces. "Look, thanks for telling me this. I know you care and I'll be careful. Okay? Let's drop the subject and talk about more interesting things."

I never told them anything more because I knew that they'd tell their parents and my parents would find out from them. That's how our culture works; the parents or older brothers find out anything they want. Some even pay their kids to spy.

I went up to my bedroom and e mailed Rafe right away.

"I hear that you're seeing another girl at the mall, and that she is a skank. I don't want you to bother me again if this is true. Just stay away… Mandhur"

That night an e mail came in from him:

"Babygirl: This is so much b s . I know exactly who told you, Tammy B., because she is so angry with Saj since he dumped her. You are the only girl I am seeing and that is the truth. Thanks for helping me, and don't listen to these gossips. They're old women who know nothing. See you tomorrow and remember who loves you! Rafe"

I deleted these messages as soon as I got them.

Rafe was most attentive the next week and I met him every afternoon in the park after school. My friends watched and said nothing more. When he left me to go home, he always met his friends at the mall. But one day, after this, he came up at lunch and said, "I need $200 today. Can you go home and get it, sweetie?"

"Two hundred? My parents will notice."

"Come on," he begged, "I really need this and I'll pay you back. What can you give me?"

"Maybe 50. You promise you'll pay it back?" I couldn't believe what I was saying.

"I need at least 75."

"It's stealing from my parents."

He grabbed me and squeezed my hand tight: "Hey, your parents have so much money, they will never notice. Think of it as a loan. They will never miss it. I thought that you cared about me." His eyes narrowed and I noticed how they glittered when he was irritated.

I nodded, "I'll try, but I can't promise. If my parents find out they will ground me forever."

He kissed me. "Get me this. They'll never know if you don't tell them."

When I met him in the park later, I gave him $20. He said, "Come on! This is crap! I said 200! I thought you were going to bring me 50, at least."

"I can't rob my own home."

"Well, then, forget it. You're so rich and your family can afford anything. I've seen your house. Five families could live in there. You're being cheap."

His friends were standing away by the swings talking. I wondered if they knew that he was asking me for money.

The next day I gave him 50 more. "Good girl," he said. "If only you could get me another 150!"

"Why do you need so much money?" I asked.

He kissed me and answered: "I can't tell you. I might get hurt."

After that, I was afraid for his safety and when he asked for money, usually 20 or 40 dollars, I stole it for him. He called it always a "loan."

Over that winter, he asked me almost every week for money. At first he'd ask for smaller amounts like $20 or $30, but gradually he started to demand larger and larger amounts. His tone became hard and rude, as if I owed it to him. I didn't know what to do. I never told anyone about this, so I couldn't ask someone what to do. I couldn't seem to say "no," particularly since he warned me that if I didn't get him the money he'd tell my parents. I was going crazy with guilt and fear that my father would find out. By spring I had given him at least $700 that I stole in little bits from my parents' box. Every dollar that I took from that box was like giving my own blood. I felt cut all over. I'd wake up, my heart thudding, thinking that this was the day they would find out and when I came home I'd be terrified that my mother or father might have discovered that money was missing. Day after day, nothing happened; they smiled at me as if everything was fine. My mother would ask how my day went; my father greeted me, "Hello, Angel." It was hard for me to look at them straight, seeing their trust in me, knowing how much I had taken from them. My perfect life had turned into a living hell.

When I finally told Rafe that I needed him to repay the money, he made excuses.

"Are you crazy? I don't have any money or I'd give it to you."

"I need it back," I said. "I stole it for you."

"Well, that was your choice. You didn't have to do that."

"What are you saying? You begged me for the money."

He looked at me then and there was a sneer on his face. "Poor little rich girl. My heart bleeds for you. But I don't have any money."

"You have to pay me soon. I want the money."

"Do you want me to rob a store or something? I don't have it."

His face looked hard and closed. Could this be the boy I loved all this year? I had given so much to him and here he was throwing it back at me. I stood there staring into space, trying to think of what to say. Lately he had been critical of me, calling me "too skinny" one day, and "stinking of onions" another. He said that I was "boring," and "a drag." Since he was such a joker, I thought that he was joking with me, but now I felt his coldness and it shocked me that he could change so fast.

"I have to split now." He walked over to Sajinder and his other friends.

I had no one to talk to since I'd stopped telling my friends anything about him once I started giving him money. I walked home with Samira, but as usual I didn't talk about Rafe,

When I got home I went up to my room and cried where no one would hear. I lay across my bed moaning softly, "What have I done?" It took a lot of discipline to come down to dinner and to act as if nothing was wrong when I was falling apart inside.

The next day, Rafe walked out of school ahead of me, and when I called for him to "Wait up," he ignored me and then turned around and shouted to this friends, "Look at that ugly girl; she keeps bothering me!" His friends glanced back at me and kept walking. I looked around to see if other students had heard him. Some girls behind me whispered to each other and stared at me like I was a leper. I ran after him, but he refused to turn around when I called him. I was yelling, "What did I do?" but they disappeared over the hill and never looked back.

That next day I went up to him as soon as I saw him.

"Rafe, what is the matter? Why did you yell at me like that yesterday? Were you joking? What's going on?"

He gave me a dirty look. "Hey, get off my case. I don't need you following me around like a ghost. Get a life, rich b   ."

"You didn't call me a rich b   when I was giving so much money."

He mumbled, "Look, sorry, but I'm with someone else."

I grabbed his jacket, "What?"

"Just let me go, okay, let me go!" He yanked the jacket out of my hand so violently it ripped and I fell down on the floor. He bolted off to join his friends, who were waiting on the street.

Suddenly, my teacher Ms. Ventura came out of the staff room and saw me lying there. "Mandhur, what are you doing there? Is everything all right?"

She helped me up, and lifted an eyebrow. "What's up?"

I wanted to tell her the truth, I was so devastated, but I remembered what my father would do if he found out. I just said, "Oh, I slipped."

She laughed. "You have to be more careful."

I nodded and went out.

The next day Samira told me that Rafe was going with one of the Grade 8 girls, Andira. She had a very mature body and went with boys from high school, but I knew that she'd had a thing for Rafe. She was always giving me the evil eye.

"Are you surprised?" Samira asked. "Forget him, please, you're too nice a girl for such an animal."

I think I could have stood it if that had been the end, but it wasn't. For weeks after that, he'd call out insults to his friends when he saw me: "She's the ugly girl, the untouchable. Don't go near her; you get a disease from that one!"

I received anonymous e mails: "Die Thief!" and "He only wanted your money. He hated you!" and "Nobody wants your disease." I guessed these were from Andira and her friends, but once again I wouldn't tell the school because I was afraid my parents would be notified.

I wanted to disappear after stealing so much from my parents and them not knowing and trusting me. I stopped eating, and couldn't sleep or concentrate. I started to carry a razor blade in my backpack. I would make little cuts on my arms that bled and every time I did this, I felt better. I had found the perfect way to punish myself and let out the pain that was building up worse every day. I didn't know what else to do. Samira knew that I was cutting and she was worried for me. "I'm fine," I told her.

In Grade 8, I had Ms. Ventura again for English. She was teaching the novel *The Giver*, which is about a society that has outlawed feelings of any kind. Anyone who feels gets sent to this room where they are killed. I loved this novel and finished it in two nights, way ahead of the class. After we had finished this, Ms. Ventura asked us to write a personal story about a time when we hid our own feelings. She added, "This is a very personal topic and I want to assure you that it will remain private and I will tell no one. But it will be read and marked by me."

I sat there at home in my bedroom wondering what to write. I was sick with shame and yet I was excited at the thought of telling what happened to me. Then I started writing and didn't stop for about three hours. You are reading now what I handed in to Ms. Ventura. I wrote, "Private, to be read by Ms. Ventura only" and I put it in a sealed envelope.

Every day after that, I watched Ms. Ventura's face to see if she looked at me differently, or had changed in any way about me. She seemed exactly the same and I wondered if she'd read it. I felt strangely excited.

A week later, she handed back the assignments. When I turned mine over, I saw her note:

Dear Mandhur:
This is a well written narrative and clearly shows the characters through their actions and dialogue. You have edited it very skillfully. Well done. 50/50
This story shows that you have enormous courage for your age.

You have been through a life changing experience that would wound and permanently damage anybody's life. By writing about it in class, however, you free yourself to acknowledge your own mistakes and show how badly you feel about your actions with Rafe and against your own parents. I know the risks involved in your writing this and I want to assure you that I will tell no one about it. However, I would like to help you to recover from this experience by talking with you at some length and possibly with the school social worker. Again, it will all remain confidential.

Please speak to me when you are ready.

Ms. Ventura

I smiled as I read her comments. I felt as if a 500 pound weight had just lifted off my shoulders. I saw the scars on my arms fading. I watched her perched on the side of her desk in her green corduroy pants and sweater, saying, "People, let's turn to Chapter 6 of our novel so we can discuss how someone escapes from this kind of society." I looked outside the window at the blue sky and colored trees and knew that I was lucky to have such a teacher that you can trust and I knew that I would talk with her as soon as she could give me the time.

On the way home, I walked with my friends and, listening to them talking, I thought "I am happy." I thought that I would never get over this. I was self destructive because no one can keep their feelings so hidden. It isn't natural. I knew, in some way I couldn't yet say, that Ms. Ventura was going to help me deal with my life. With that hope, I went home that day to my family.

Commentary

Mandhur's story is the kind you rarely hear, because, typically, the student is terrified that their family will find out. This is particularly true of some religious immigrant students, but it is also true for most other students, bullies and victims alike. Mandhur's story is important because it reflects the kinds of pressures that kids are living with and shows how those pressures make them think and act. These students often suffer a lot of guilt and anguish as a result of living between two cultures (their own and Canadian). Some students would never be physically safe if their parents found out they were disobeying their cultural and religious norms. Some have even had to leave home and assume different identities, because they feared for their lives.

Perhaps what is most shocking in this story is that Mandhur is a bright and attractive student, who is popular with staff and students. She comes from an affluent and close-knit family, whom she respects and fears. Yet, for some reason, she is drawn towards a manipulative boy and becomes a thief and a liar in order to keep his approval. She is a very strong person who tries to work things out on her own, but learns that she has to tell her story to someone. This is very hard for most kids to accept. They will stay silent about the most devious, hurtful experiences out of loyalty to their parents and friends. Most kids would rather die than hurt their parents by telling them about some shameful act.

Fortunately, teachers can help by being non judgmental in the way they teach and listen to their students. Most stories studied in classrooms concern the theme of justice in some way. By highlighting the theme of justice and by getting kids to think, talk, and write about justice in their own lives and relationships, teachers can help kids communicate about the issues they are struggling with at home and in the community. Such classes provide students with a place to create their own vision of how the world should be and what they should be getting out of it. Many students live in emotionally repressive homes, where it is dangerous to tell what you are feeling or thinking. School can be a place where kids find some way of dealing with these problems. Teachers need to be trained to engage students in this kind of connection and understanding, whether they teach literature, geography, history, science, religion, health, or gym.

Questions for discussion
(For adults and older teens)

1. Have you ever done something for someone that you were ashamed of and could never tell your parents/family about? How did this affect your life? How have you resolved this experience?

2. Have you ever been manipulated in a relationship? How did you resolve this? What would you do if you had a second chance with this situation?

Activities
(For students)

1. Name five of the most important rules in your family. How do you follow these?

2. Tell or write a story about a time when you didn't follow one or more of these rules and show what the repercussions were.

3. Have you ever been bullied in a relationship? How did you handle this? Could you discuss this with your parents? Why? Why not? Write or discuss your answer.

4
Justin

"I just want to be a peacemaker."

He looks so normal to me now, in his baseball cap and sweatshirt, like he could be almost… any kid. Whew, it feels good to think that.

A year ago, if I saw Brendan coming, my heart would start pounding. I'd get butterflies in my stomach and look away, hoping he wouldn't notice me. My friends would ask what was wrong, but my tongue would stick to the roof of my mouth and I couldn't talk. That was in Grade 4.

Brendan seemed to know this, because he mostly picked on me. He and his friend Tyler would usually butt in to our group in the schoolyard and he'd start saying stuff like, "Hey stupid," his eyes glinting at me, and Tyler would laugh this stupid laugh as if it were so funny, and if I said, "Knock it off, Brendan," or anything in protest, he'd always sneer, "I was just foolin', dummy," as if I were the one who'd done something wrong. My friends would laugh, too, even when they knew I didn't like it. It was like they were afraid, too, so they made like it was all a joke, except he'd been doing it to me since Grade 2.

I tried to ignore it and not let him bother me, hoping it would stop. But he'd get worse, as if he couldn't stand me not reacting. Once, we were playing baseball in our class and he landed on my first base and actually started pushing against me saying, "Move over, move over." I knew he was trying to start something, trying to stir me up. I wouldn't react; I wasn't going to let him control me. That made him worse. He'd call me "loser," "gay," or "retard," no matter what I did.

I wondered why. Why is Brendan still picking on me? Why doesn't he pick on Matthew or Simon or somebody else? I think he couldn't stand that I was different, that I didn't get mad and mean about everything that happened like he did. Or maybe he didn't like that I am popular and I do attract friends because I am fun and I don't put others down.

Every day that fall was tough because he wouldn't let up. Once, my backpack went missing for half the day. I was going crazy asking everyone if they'd seen it because my science project that I made was in it. Then he comes up to me with it after lunch "Hey, Justin, is this your backpack? I found it on the field." He gave this little smile and I knew that he'd taken it and hidden it outside before school started. "Oh, I wondered whose it was."

I knew that he'd taken it from the floor where I'd dropped it beside my desk, but I couldn't prove it. A few days later he started this rumor that I had leukemia. I had this little rash on my cheek from a food allergy and he went around and told everyone that I had cancer! All these kids were looking at me strange and then my friend Matthew asked me if it was true what Brendan was saying, that I had leukemia. "What?" I almost yelled. "Why do you listen to him? He doesn't know anything."

At recess I walked over to Brendan and told him to stop spreading stories that weren't true. He made a face and said it wasn't him; one of the girls had said it. "Who?" I demanded, but he wouldn't say.

I told our teacher Mr. Marchese that someone was spreading a story that I had cancer and it wasn't true. He didn't ask, but I didn't want to say that it was Brendan because I knew that Brendan would deny it anyway. When I went home I felt lousy and Matthew said, "He's a jerk; don't let him bother you."

At supper that night I ate a bit of pasta and garlic bread. Then I didn't want anything else and just sat there playing with the salt and peppers. My mum asked, "What's the matter? Aren't you hungry?"

I just blurted it: "There's this kid at school who's always bugging me, trying to get me in some way."

"Is it Brendan again?" she asked. "I told you last year to ignore him. That boy just wants attention."

My dad chewed and swallowed some bread: "What's he been doing now?"

When I told him, Dad said, "Brendan is a bully; I can tell because I was bullied a bit when I was your age – by a girl no less. She beat me up every day, until I just ignored her and stopped running away."

He gave me some advice. "Don't let the bully know that you notice or care and he'll give up, I promise you." Mom agreed: "Yes, that's all he wants. Attention. Don't let him bother you. Have you done that?"

"Yes," I answered. "I've been ignoring it, but he's trying every day to get me mad. I don't want to fight; I don't want to be like him."

"And you shouldn't," my mum said. "You should not let this boy affect you. Have you told your teacher?"

"Yeah, but I didn't say who it was cause I know Brendan will deny it and say I'm picking on him. That's what he did in Grade 2."

My little sister Emily said that she told the teacher on any bully in her class. I said, "Yeah, but you're a girl."

My mum sighed, "Well, we could see the teacher or the principal again. We hate to see you so disturbed by this kid."

I pushed my chair back from the table and stood up.

"No! I don't want you to see the teacher or principal. That will make it worse. He'll just do it more and more. I know that. There's this kid Nathan who kids are calling 'Gaylord' because he's no good in sports and stuff and his father came to the office to complain and kids are even worse now, calling him really bad stuff and mimicking him because he can't even run straight or throw a ball."

My parents shook their heads. "Well, we want to help, but you seem to think we can't do anything. We support you, but if this is affecting you so much we'll have to do something."

My mother added, "Brendan's parents don't seem to want to know what he is doing. I remember calling his mum back in Grade 2 and she pretty well told me to mind my own business – that Brendan didn't pick on kids. Remember? She said that *you* were the troublemaker."

"That's why Brendan thinks he can do this. His mum protects him."

"But," my mum said, looking me in the eye, "you don't have to let him bother you. Nobody makes you feel bad without your permission. Remember that. You have that power."

It helped to talk with my parents, but I still I wasn't sleeping well at night. I'd wake up from nightmares about these werewolves chasing me. At school I tried to ignore Brendan and pretend that he wasn't there. It was hard because he was in my class.

Then a week later, on Pizza Day, my friends and I were sitting together in the cafeteria eating our slices. Brendan and Tyler zoomed up to us and ate their pizzas with us. When Brendan finished, he threw his pizza crust across the room into the garbage bin. He yelled "Bingo" when he hit the basket and then without warning he took my pop and started to open it.

"Hey, that's mine," I said. He dropped my pop and placed his hands around my neck and started tightening his hold. It was like he was going to strangle me. "Stop that," I choked.

He laughed like a maniac and dropped his hands. "Don't you know anything? I was kidding."

I wanted to tell Mrs. Spanner the cafeteria supervisor, but I knew that would make him worse. He wanted to get me and I wasn't going to let him do that.

I decided to tell my teacher, Mr. Marchese, one afternoon when I stayed late to talk with him. He's a pretty cool teacher and coaches track and field, so I started talking to him about spring training because I run the relay. Then I just said, "Brendan is always bothering me."

"What's he doing?" Mr. Marchese swung around on his chair and stood up. His brown eyes were friendly enough. I didn't want him to think that I was a tattler who couldn't look after myself.

I cleared my throat and answered, "He's trying to make me mad by taking stuff, pushing me around, calling me names. Telling stories about me that aren't true."

"When did this start?"

"Two years ago."

"Why didn't you report it before?"

I thought about this and replied, "Well, I did way back in Grade 2, but he denied all the things that I said he did. So I've tried to ignore him. I didn't want to make it worse. I didn't want to be a tattle tale."

I knew Mr. Marchese believed me because he said that he'd speak to Brendan.

But when Mr. Marchese asked him the next morning, Brendan lied and said that I was making it all up and he was acting in self defense and Mr. Marchese told us that we should both visit the principal's office to settle our grievances. When we were outside the room, Brendan said, "Loser!"

The main office was just down the hall from the class. On the way, Brendan whispered, "You're going to get it for this. You're makin' trouble for me, dork."

I didn't answer and then I said, "I'm sick of your stupid games."

He laughed like it was a big joke.

I looked out the glass front doors as we passed them. It was a snowy day and I wished I could have run out the door and gone home.

Mrs. Walcott, our principal, met us in the office. "What's going on with you boys? You're not usually in here," she smiled behind her red square glasses. "Come on in and talk." She led us into her office. It was full of photographs of her family, and stuffed animals, and there was a big glass jar of jujubes on the table. She didn't offer us any.

She just sat behind her desk and asked, "Who's going to go first?"

Brendan had this troubled look on his face. "I will. Justin is bothering me all the time. He starts trouble, saying that I poked him, or I took his stuff when I didn't, or that I swore and called him names."

I just stared at him as he went on and Mrs. Walcott listened. "Like I never did that. Him and his friends… they don't like me. They're trying to get me in trouble." I wanted to speak out, but Mrs. Walcott silenced me to wait my turn. Brendan was making this all up and Mrs. Walcott believed him. Finally, she turned to me and said, "What's your side of things, Justin?"

I didn't know what to say at first, then I told her, "Brendan's lying. None of this happened. I never picked on him or took his stuff. He's always making fun of me and calling me names."

Brendan was shaking his head. "No way, uh uh, I never did that."

Mrs. Walcott lifted her eyebrows. "Well, I don't know who to believe. You both seem to be at fault because you're accusing each other of the same things. I want you boys to leave each other alone. Don't touch, don't go near each other. Do you understand me?"

We both nodded and Brendan smiled, "Thanks, Mrs. Walcott."

I hurried back to the class and let Brendan saunter down the hall alone.

When I walked home with my friends that night I told them how Brendan fooled the principal. They agreed that he was a big phoney. When we got to his house, Matthew said, "You have to just ignore him; he's bad news, you know. He's just jealous that you have more friends than him and that you're a better baseball player." I asked Matthew and Simon if they'd tell the principal their side of things so she'd know that Brendan was lying. They looked at each other and shifted their feet, as if they were embarrassed. Then Matthew coughed and shook his head, "Like, he doesn't really pick on me and I don't want to start anything with him."

Simon looked down. "My mum told me not to get involved with Brendan. I don't think she'd let me speak to the principal."

Matthew looked uneasy. He touched my shoulder. "Just leave him alone. It's not worth getting upset about, you know what I mean."

"Yeah," added Simon. "Let's not talk about him anymore."

"Okay, you guys," I said, and went home.

After that, I did what the principal said and ignored him, no matter what. For a while, Brendan left me alone, too, but then he started making faces, mouthing insults, smirking at anything I did.

It was all sneaky, only I seemed to notice, that's how clever he was. After a month or two, though, he started laughing out loud if I got a low mark on anything, calling me "a dummy" when I said the wrong answer in class, or "a goof" when I fumbled once in soccer.

I ignored him as best I could, but things bothered me. Little things. I was always looking over my shoulder to check if someone was following me. I got jumpy over a car backfiring, or a dogfight in the park. I had to check and recheck my backpack to make sure all my stuff was there. When I washed up, I always scrubbed my hands two or three times in case I might get a disease. I hung out with my friends at school, but I never told them any of these things. I didn't want anyone to know.

I didn't talk to my mom before supper in the kitchen anymore. I just went down and started my homework or watched TV. I told Emily to "Shut up, stupid," and pushed her off when she sat too close on the couch when I watching. I told her to "Go away!" when she kept asking me to play *Monopoly*. Then I just hung out in my room, listening to music, playing on my computer.

I even lost my appetite; I just wasn't hungry, even when we had my favorite food, chicken cashew stir fry. I didn't want to talk at family meetings when my parents asked us how things were going.

At school, I pretended that Brendan didn't exist. I imagined him being changed into a toad, or vanishing when a powder was poured over him. I imagined him dead and buried in a grave 50 feet under the earth. Nobody knew that he still bothered me and that made him worse. One day I came to my desk and I saw some words scrawled on it. I looked closely and read "Justin = gay." I knew right away who wrote it and I rubbed it out before anyone else could read it. After that I saw other words, like "DingBat!!!" and swear words that I would never put on my desk. I rubbed these off, too. I just knew that he'd deny it if I told and the teacher might think that I had written them.

My nightmares came back. The same werewolf was hiding in my house, waiting till dark to come upstairs and get me. It had red eyes and jagged fangs and shaggy fur. I'd wake up shaking, certain that it was in my room. My mum heard me and came in. "What's wrong, Justin?"

"I thought there was something there," I whispered. "That's all."

The next day she said, "Come here and sit down. I want to visit with you."

I kept looking away. When she tried to hug me, I pushed her off and ran to my room. "LEAVE ME ALONE!!" I shouted through the door.

I went and crossed off another day on my calendar. Somehow that helped me, seeing only 90 more days and I'd be free of Brendan. I picked up my new Harry Potter book and started reading. I wished that Dumbledore would come and cast a spell over Brendan.

A bit later Mum knocked on the door. I wouldn't answer it and she spoke quietly. "I am so worried about you. You're changing, you're becoming a different boy. I'm afraid. Please let me come in."

I opened the door and said, "It doesn't matter. You can't do anything to help."

"Well, I can tell you that you are my son, my beautiful son, and you are being twisted up by this kid. You can't let Brendan affect you like this. Why can't you show him what you feel?"

"I don't want to be like him. I don't want to fight him. That's what he wants, Mum; he wants me to be like him and I won't be."

"But you're actually worse," she replied, "because you're bottling this all up. It's making you mean and tense. Look at your face. It's all tense and wrinkled like an old man's. You're so upset, darling."

"I don't want to fight." I clenched my fists.

My mum said, "Sometimes you have to fight to show someone that you mean what you say. It's better than bottling this up inside you."

That night she came into my room and propped up a photo by my bed. "What's that?" I asked. She was covering it with her hand, then drew her hand away.

"That's you when you were 18 months old. Look at you, full of light and life and love. My lovely baby, full of eagerness. Look at your eyes."

I looked away from the photograph.

"I'm going to leave it here for you to look at when you want to see who you are deep inside," she continued.

I turned over and faced the wall so I didn't have to kiss her good night. She bent over and kissed my back.

"Good night," she said.

Dad came in a few minutes later. "Hey there, sport, how's it going?"

"Okay, I guess," I said, turning over in bed.

"How's things at school? You've been kind of quiet lately. Is Brendan minding his own business?

"Yeah, I guess. Things are okay."

"Well, you be sure to let us know what's happening."

"Yeah sure."

Dad sat down on my bed. "I was thinking that maybe you and I could plan a little hiking trip this weekend. I'd like to go out to the mountain and walk some of those trails. How about it?"

"Okay. Is the rest of the family coming?"

"I thought that we'd make it a guy's day trip."

"Okay."

"That's a nice photo of you there. I remember you had such a great imagination. You made all the sounds for all the animals, and birds too. You were such a happy little guy."

I looked at the photo. I was sitting in the garden with our cat, laughing about something. I had a lot of short curls.

"Good night, Justin."

Dad rubbed my shoulders a little and hugged me.

"Good night, Dad"

Each day the little photo sat by my bed and I looked at it when I woke up and before I went to sleep. The little boy looked so happy and fearless. He looked like someone I'd like to know.

Mum came in to say good night at night. She looked at the photo and said, "I hope you reconnect with that child, because you know that's you!"

For some weird reason, my eyes filled up and I couldn't speak.

Dad and I went hiking on the Saturday. It was a dry, clear day, though cool, and we did the longer two hour trail that wound through the mountain. There were lots of broken trees that had fallen in the winter storms. "They were probably dead already," my dad commented.

We found wolf tracks and woodpecker holes on the trees.

Mostly we walked in silence and listened to the wind whistling in the treetops. The old trees creaked.

At the top we sat and ate our sandwiches and drank our water. My dad sat looking out across the mountain: "There are always going to be bullies, people who think it's fun to push others around. Why, I know adults like that. You can't change them, so it's best to ignore them and stay out of their way. But you can't let them get away with this; you have to show some strength."

"I don't want to fight, Dad," I said. "There's too much war in the world. I just want to be a peacemaker."

"That's a great ambition, but it means, then, that you have to be very strong inside and not let a bully get to you the way you've let Brendan. You need to realize that not everyone is like you and you have to be able to accept that there are other positions besides yours."

We came down the mountain and drove home. When I went upstairs, I looked at the photo my mother had given me. The little boy in the picture wasn't afraid of anything. He looked like he could conquer the world.

I lay down on my bed. I wanted to feel that way again. I was tired of this suffering. I closed my eyes and imagined myself walking to school. I saw Brendan and he was taunting me as usual. But instead of being disturbed I saw myself expanding, getting bigger and taller, with long curly hair, and laughing as I walked in the sun. Brendan started to shrink, growing smaller until he was a little midget jumping up and down, and shouting insults in a tiny voice that was impossible to hear. I kept on walking towards my friends and he scurried out of my way. As I lay there, I knew that Brendan was just a kid who was so unhappy he had to put his misery on me, to make me the same as him. And I laughed because now I knew that it didn't matter at all. I was strong and imaginative and I had my own inner visions and no one outside of me could change that.

When I opened my eyes, I knew that Brendan was never going to hurt me again because I would never accept inside what he was saying.

I remembered my mom saying that "no one can make you feel bad without your permission."

She was right. I had been giving Brendan permission to make me feel bad about myself. When I stood up, I knew that he'd never get that permission again.

It's funny, it didn't happen overnight, but by the end of May, Brendan's influence just faded away like a genie back into a bottle. I went back to school with my own invisible shield, my peacemaker – which is partly my baby photo, but also my beliefs in nature and world peace and stuff like that – and no one but me knows why he doesn't bother me anymore.

Somehow, though, Brendan knew, because he pretty well gave up picking on me by the start of Grade 5.

Commentary

Justin's story shows that no matter how sensitive and caring their families may be, children find it almost impossible to tell their parents, let alone their teachers or school principals, what a bully is doing. Part of this resistance to telling is based on shame; children are ashamed about being the target of bullying. The resistance also arises because they believe there must be something wrong with them or else they wouldn't be bullied. And, of course, many children believe that, if they tell, the bully will get even and make it even worse for them.

This story also shows that parents and principals cannot rescue kids from bullies, regardless of how much they want to. Bullies are clever at concealing their activities and a lot of the worst bullying is psychological and almost invisible to adults. It consists of looks, gestures, mouthed words, taunts, and jibes, which are often done in a sneaky and backbiting manner. When physical bullying *does* occur, the typical response from the bully is, "I was only fooling," making the victim look like a loser who doesn't have a sense of humor, or who can't read people right.

Justin is typical of a boy who is an individual and who, at nine years of age, already has a firm sense of his own values and beliefs. Children like him are often targeted precisely because they *are* individuals who stand out in the crowd for their independence and idealism. They also don't want to fight or be aggressive, as it goes against their ideals. A bully can make such a child's life hell, as Brendan did with Justin.

Since Brendan's parents are not cooperative, it becomes very difficult for the school and the parents to do anything to stop him. Justin is fortunate that his mother and father have great respect for him and don't shut him up with advice, but offer what they can and wait with vigilance to see what happens. When his mother sees him changing for the worse, she places a baby photo by his bed, to remind him of who he really is. This benign assistance is helpful because Brendan can look at it when he wants to and can think about how his 18 month old self connects to his nine year old self. Then, through spending some time alone with his dad, Justin is able to connect with his deeper self and find the strength he needs to develop an inner shield that will protect him from Brendan. Ironically, he is able to develop an inner warrior stance to support his peacemaker personality. In real life, this might take some months, but the steps shown here are ones that could help a child.

Activities and questions for discussion
(For adults or youths in small or large groups)

1. Tell or write about a time when you were bullied. Show where it happened and how you felt. Show how you stopped it.
2. Write or tell about a time when you were a bully. Show where it happened and what you did. Show how you felt and how you stopped.
3. Describe the personal ideals and beliefs that give you strength and confidence in yourself.
4. Show how you keep a positive sense of yourself when you are around others, without putting them down.
5. Write a story, poem, or paint a picture that shows your inner beliefs.

5
Catelyn

"My friends and I thought we were cool."

I never thought that I was a bully before that spring day when the vice principal, Mr. Sullivan, called me out of class to his office. I wondered what it was about, thinking that he probably wanted me to work on a project again like the Christmas basket drive, but he didn't seem too pleasant when I sat down in front of him. He was frowning and his eyes looked cool as they searched mine. He glanced down at his notes and began speaking in a clipped tone: "Catelyn, I asked to see you to find out about the e mails you've been sending to a certain girl in this school."

My heart started pounding. "Who are you talking about?"

"Melissa Henry."

"She's in my home form and a couple of classes, but I don't really know her."

"Yet you sent her a number of e mails."

"I don't remember sending e mails to her directly; it might have been part of a list to a bunch of people and she got it sent to her in a big mailing, but I never sent her a personal e mail."

"Do you have a problem with your memory?"

"My computer memory?"

"You know what I mean – your own memory, because you *did* send Melissa what I'd call a one of a kind message."

"No, I am sure I didn't."

Mr. Sullivan stared at me for a moment. Neither of us spoke. Then he said, "I am finding this very hard. You are, in many ways, an outstanding student. You're one of the best hockey players in the city, and an outstanding athlete in the junior school. To discover this... is most disappointing."

I shrugged my shoulders, "If I knew what you were talking about…"

He handed me some papers, printouts of MSN messages. My cybername, "chocobaby," was on the address. How did Sullivan get these? I looked up, "These were private messages meant for friends."

"Right. And Melissa was one of your recipients, and you wrote some pretty nasty messages to her, wouldn't you agree?"

"Well, I… I… I didn't do it on my own; there was a bunch of us who used my MSN address. I… we didn't intend any harm."

Mr. Sullivan glared at me. "You have an answer for everything, even for this kind of mean and stupid message, which you admit you sent."

"My friends and I did, as a joke," I said.

His eyes narrowed: "Oh, and this message here telling her to kill herself or somebody else will is just a joke? And this one telling her that her 'butt is so big everybody laughs at you when you walk by.' Or this one, 'You are so ugly that even the biggest losers wouldn't be seen with you.' Hello? What kind of joke is this?"

Silence.

"Well, what do you have to say for yourself?"

I didn't answer. I couldn't speak. I looked out the window. Some kids who were skipping class were smoking, all huddling together on the sidewalk, just off school property.

"Melissa's mother was just here this morning to tell us that last weekend Melissa tried to take her own life. They were able to save her and take her to Emergency. They discovered that these messages, which you sent over the past month, put her over the edge. She was terrified to let her parents know, in case they came to the school and you were found out. But she will not be returning to this school after today and her mother wants to make sure that this doesn't happen to someone else. The principal is talking to her parents now, and then she'll see you, but I am advising you that you are facing suspension and possibly worse. I don't think that you have any idea how serious this is."

"It was a bunch of us," I muttered.

"We'll get to them later. From what we've learned from some... other students, you are the ringleader. As well, some students have reported being harassed by you, and that you have influenced others to support you, even when it's wrong."

I felt as if a ton of bricks was falling down on me as he spoke. My head started aching.

"The principal has called your mother and father, who I gather are at work."

"My mother and father?"

"Of course. They have to be informed. The police are also being contacted by Melissa's parents. This kind of hate mail is against the safe school act."

The whole world was turning against me. I stared at the floor, my mind in a blur. How could this be happening? I was a good student, popular enough, planning on becoming a lawyer. I didn't need a bad student record. I was counting on a sports scholarship to a big university. The police?! My parents would freak if they got a call about this. I couldn't believe that Melissa tried to kill herself. What would I say to the principal?

Mr. Sullivan was speaking again. "Could you repeat that?" I asked.

"I was wondering if you wanted to talk to me about it before you see the principal."

The period bell went and the smokers came inside. I guess I wasn't going back to class.

"I don't know what to say."

"Why do you think you are a bully?"

"I'm not a bully."

"Well, what do you call all these messages to Melissa, if not bullying? Telling her no one likes her, that she is ugly, and should die?"

"I've never hurt an... an... animal or a little kid or anyone. I babysit a lot and the parents say I'm one of the best sitters they've had."

"Attacking a person with words is as damaging as using a knife, and most people carry those taunts for the rest of their lives like a scar. You are a bully and a dangerous one precisely because you don't know that you are one."

"I never scare anyone."

"That's where you're wrong. Your messages have scared a number of students who are staying away from school or avoiding having anything to do with you. Why do you think they're afraid of you?"

"Who? Who are these students?" I asked.

"I am not telling you any names because you might try to get them for reporting," Mr. Sullivan replied. "I'm trying to discover why you do this to other students. What's your problem? Why are you so hostile?"

I didn't answer. I was imagining my mother's face as she heard the principal tell her about what I'd done. My mother would suck in her breath and her eyes would pop, and then she'd say, "Do you want me to come to the school now?" I could see her charging in: "What's this all about?"

"I don't know!" is what I'd tell her.

I remembered the day I met Melissa. The teacher had introduced her as "a new girl from Halifax." She stood there, tall, with big eyes and long brown hair, wearing tight jeans and a little navy blue sweater, with shiny lip gloss on her lips.

From the start, she didn't want to be friends with girls. Later that week, in a spare period, she asked my boyfriend, Jason, if he could help her with the math homework because it was all different from what they did in Halifax. She asked him the next day and the next, and she started to hang out with this rich snob, Tracy, who nobody liked. They never hung in the hall before class, unless boys like Kevin, or Jason and Derrick were standing there already. Even though Jason said she was "just a friend," I figured she had other ideas, and my friends Jessica and Roxann and I dropped an anonymous note into her locker, warning her to "leave him alone or else watch out."

Melissa ignored the warnings and kept on asking Jason for help. A few weeks later, we sent a few e-mails telling her that she didn't look so good. "Your lip gloss stinks of rotten fruit" and "your legs are thick sticks." I sent a couple on my own: "Why don't you drop dead… nobody cares about you, sl--."

As I sat in the vice principal's office, I wondered how Melissa guessed it was us, since we never signed out names.

I also wondered who else had told on us. Who could it be? We made fun of a lot of kids in the school, just little stuff, letting off steam, that's all. Apart from Melissa, we never meant any of it. There was Suzanne, the ugly goth girl; nobody liked her. She wore black… *everything*: skirts, stockings, boots, top, lipstick, eyeliner, hair dye. She was so pathetic she cut her arms with a razor and then wore short sleeves or transparent shirts so that others could see the scars. We sent her some e-mails telling her to "die already… just do it… nobody will miss you." She always excused herself in French class to go to the washroom and one day Roxann caught her cutting herself in there. The next day I also got excused and sat in the cubicle next to her and whispered, "Hey, Cutter Girl, why don't you just cut your wrists or your throat? Go on, *do* it." She didn't come out while I was there, but she probably knew that it was me. Would she have reported that?

There were other kids, too, like Henry, the psycho who sat beside me in English class. He had to take meds for Tourette's syndrome or something, and couldn't sit up in his seat for a whole period. Because I sat beside him, I was his partner all the time and had to do all the work myself. I used to call him "Schizo," "Freak," "Retard," and he'd look at me with this dumbest face, like he was asking for it. I think he liked the attention.

And there was that tall Filipino gay, Toy, who wore perfume and wanted to be a model. But we weren't the only kids who teased him; the guys hit on him outside the school, in the corridors, and cafeteria. Sometimes I felt sorry for him; he had no friends but girls. But I don't think the principal heard from any of those kids. They'd never tell; they're such losers. They'd be too afraid…

Mr. Sullivan snapped his fingers before my eyes. "Catelyn, do you have anything more to say?"

"I wasn't the only one," I replied. "Lots of kids pick on people at this school. It can be brutal. I am sorry about Melissa, but I don't see why it's all coming down on me."

Mr. Sullivan stood up and straightened his tie. "I think we better go down to see the principal. Come along with me."

We walked down to the main office. The principal's door was closed. Her secretary, Ms. DaVito said, "Take a seat. She'll be out in a moment."

Mr. Sullivan left me there and returned to his office. I saw other kids lined up outside. Some teachers and students passing in and out of the office glanced over at me, but I stared straight ahead and out the windows, listening to the sounds of the grass mower as the janitors worked on the grounds.

When my mother walked in, she was breathless. She looked around, but didn't see me sitting on the bench. "Hey, Mom," I said, as I got up and walked over to her. She wasn't wearing lipstick and her mascara had smeared into the corners of her eyes. "What's going on?" she hissed.

"Nothing, like, that I did. This kid Melissa tried to kill herself and her mom is blaming it on me."

"Well, the principal tells a different story and wants to suspend you for e-mailing and picking on students in this school. I had to take off from work early and I was in a very important meeting when she called. Your father's going to kill you for this and don't smile like that. This is not funny."

"I never did any of the things they're saying."

The principal's door opened and Melissa and her parents walked out. She was pale and leaning against them but looked away when she saw me. Mrs. MacDonald, the principal, asked us in and closed the door. She motioned us to sit down in two black leather chairs while she went and sat behind her huge desk.

"Well, this is a shock," she said. "Catelyn, you are on our student council and athletic teams. You and the other students did a wonderful job on the basket drive at Christmas. We know now that you have damaged some of our students in cruel ways. Why are you such an aggressive student?"

She stared at me across the desk and waited.

"Catelyn says that she didn't send any e-mails or attack other students. What evidence do you have to show this?" my mother asked.

Mrs. MacDonald handed my mother a file on her desk. "You'll find it all here… her e-mails, reports of attacks on this student…"

"But who said this?" I asked her. "I want to know who's setting me up?" I started crying as my mother read through the papers in the file. "I don't understand any of this."

My mother looked up. "It looks like you wrote these from our computer: "Die, sl--"? "Your legs look like thick sticks"?

"That was a joke," I said, waving my hand at the papers. "That's the way everyone jokes here. We didn't mean anything serious! Melissa took it the wrong way."

Mrs. MacDonald shook her head. "Well, I am afraid that you are not telling the truth here. You have actually targeted students in this school and made a… a sort of campaign to destroy them. I've received a number of reports this morning from the guidance office that confirm this. Students have complained about you, among others, but you seem to be the leader. What I'd like to know is why? What makes you want to hurt other students like this?"

I looked at my mother, but she said nothing.

Then she turned to me. "Catelyn, listen, this is serious."

Mrs. MacDonald looked at me and said, "I'm suspending you for three days, and warning you that if it happens again, you will be expelled from this school. Do you understand? I also suggest that you get a good counselor." She looked at my mother. "I have a list of names of excellent counselors here that you can pick from. You will have to pay for this service, but I do recommend that you get her this help. She needs it." She handed her a paper.

We stood up to leave. I didn't speak or look up as my mother spoke.

"Well, this is all news to me. I never realized that Catelyn was doing any of this. Her father and I thought that she was doing well. Her report mentioned nothing like this."

Mrs. MacDonald shook my mother's hand and nodded at me. "Well, we all just found out ourselves; students keep things hidden from staff. Melissa showed real courage in coming forward. I hope you will consider the consequences of your actions for all concerned here, Catelyn."

All the way home my mother kept asking, "Why? What's the matter with you? Why would you do this to other kids?"

"I'm not the only one, Mom. Lots of kids diss others, but they didn't get caught." I turned my Walkman on.

"Turn that off. Well, what's wrong with the school that they can let things go so far? And while you stay home you can do some housework and stay off the phone, the computer, and that damn Walkman! Take it out of your ears now, I said. And turn off your cell phone! You start thinking about what you've done." She stopped talking after we picked up my brother Martin from his after-school program.

When we got home, I went up to my room and stayed there for the rest of the night. I opened my door a bit, when I heard her and my father arguing. He shouted, "Why would she do this?"

My mom answered, "You'd help a lot more if you took more interest in your kids."

"I'm out there trying to make things better for everybody here, what are you talking about?" He banged something with his fist and all the china clattered.

My brother started to cry and Mom said, "See, you frightened him."

I wanted to scream, "Shutup, shutup, shutup!!" to break the tension. I couldn't wait until I could leave home – only two more years. I thought about where I'd live (another city), where I'd study. Thinking about it helped to calm me down. While I was sitting there imagining my own apartment, my parents called me to supper.

"I'm not hungry," I shouted.

"Come down anyway," my dad called.

When I finally sat down at the table, my dad was almost finished eating. "So what happened? Why would you write these hate messages to other kids? Huh?"

"It wasn't hate, it was a joke, okay? We were kidding around."

"Do you think it's funny to make fun of gay students or those who are different?"

"We didn't mean it as an insult."

"What did you mean it as?"

"A funny statement, trying to make humor. Like a stand-up makes humor at other people's expense."

My dad looked at me closely. "You know, Catelyn, making fun of people off the comedy stage is considered nasty. Do you enjoy being mean to others?"

"Dad!" I said.

My mother rolled her eyes. "I wonder if you were insulted by somebody and didn't want to tell. Did somebody make a comment about your skin color?"

My mom was remembering how in grade school kids used to call me names and do mean things, like asking everyone but me to their birthday party because I was the only black kid. I used to come home and cry my eyes out. But that stopped a long time ago.

"Uh, no, everyone's like from somewhere else at that school. It's like the United Nations," I said.

"But you know how much it hurt when someone made fun of something you couldn't change," reminded my father. "You didn't like it if anyone made racial remarks to you, did you?"

I looked at him and shook my head. "Well, there are these dumb kids at school who call everybody by racial slurs. They'd never try it on me; they wouldn't dare."

My mom said, "Maybe that's what made you attack these kids? Maybe you were getting back for what happened?" She looked hopeful and angry at the same time, perhaps trying to find an excuse for my actions.

I thought about my friends and how we laughed ourselves silly when we sent these e-mails and teased these pathetic kids. We thought we were the cool people; we never thought that what we were doing was bad or wrong. It just seemed fun. I never thought that what happened in Grade 4 could affect me now.

I looked at the photograph of my grandparents that was sitting on the TV. I remembered their stories of growing up in one of the few black families in their town, and of being chased home by kids shouting out hateful words and racial slurs almost every day. But that was the old days, wasn't it? Nowadays everybody was from somewhere else and left everybody alone. And yet... could my parents be right? I always believed in thinking positive things about myself and I didn't like to remember the past. But now, I suddenly flashed back to Grade 4 and the white Maple Leaf hockey shirt that I had wanted so badly and finally received for Christmas. How I loved it – the white satiny shirt with its bright blue maple leaf and stripes. I wore it to skate in the park across from my house and some kids I always played with said, "Yo, don't you know? Black kids can't wear a white Leafs shirt! Take it off!" They threw dirt on it to mark it up and made stains that never came out, no matter how hard my mom scrubbed. They tried to stop me from wearing it; every time I came out in it they'd shout "n-----, take it off." I remembered the day I hauled off and beat two of them up I was that mad. I kept wearing that shirt till it was old and fell apart, and every time I wore it, I pledged that nobody would ever make me feel bad again.

After that, I picked on any kid before they could pick on me and kids respected me.

It all happened so long ago that I'd almost forgotten about it.

"Maybe you're right," I said finally. "Maybe I got too good at defending myself and I just forgot what it feels like to be bullied." I felt weak like I was going to fall over. I went up to my room and went right to bed and slept till the next morning. When I got up, I found a note from my parents telling me to do my homework and not go out.

I spent the morning doing homework and then, though my parents told me not to, I rang Jason on his cell phone.

"Hey," he said, when he answered it.

"Hi," I said.

"Whazzup?" he asked.

I realized he didn't know I'd been suspended and when I told him he got quiet and didn't speak. "Jason," I said, "*say* something."

A minute ticked by and I heard someone laughing. He said, "Shhh."

"Jason, what's going on? Who are you with?"

Silence. Then he spoke. "Uh, look, uh, I don't know how to say this, but we're like over. I wanted to tell you in person, but I found out about Melissa and I thought it was gross... and uh..."

"Jason?" He didn't answer. "What's going on? Speak to me."

"Uh... look, Catelyn, I don't want to talk about it... there's nothing to say."

"Why? I need to know, especially now."

"Well, when I heard what happened to Melissa and that you sent her all those crappy messages... I thought it was a totally rotten thing to do... uh, I just don't want to be with... you."

"Jason?" I wanted to explain how it was a joke, but he hung up.

I called Roxann. She was in class. "I'll call you back."

At lunch she called and said, "They're calling lots of kids down to the office and asking a lot of questions. It's scary," she said.

"I got suspended," I told her.

"Omigod, that's bad. My mother will kill me if I get suspended."

"Do you know what Jason is doing?"

"Yeah, he's not speaking to us."

"Why?"

"I think he heard about Melissa and blames us. That's what kids are saying, that we drove her to suicide."

"I have to go now," I said.

I felt sick all over, hearing that Jason was so angry. I wished I could disappear into a black hole in the earth and never come out again. It seemed like my whole life was going up in smoke and all my popularity had blown away.

I sat down and started to write a letter to Melissa. It seemed the only way to stop feeling so bad.

Dear Melissa,

I know that you have been very sick and I hope that you are feeling better. I am sorry for the dumb way that I picked on you and I hope that you realize that me and my friends were just fooling and didn't mean anything serious.

You probably think that sounds weird, but I am telling you the truth. A long time ago, in Grades 2–4, kids used to make fun and insult me because of my color. It really hurt and one day I decided that I would become a tough popular kid so that it would never happen again.

I am wishing now that I could take back all the words I said to you, because I didn't mean them.

I hope that your new school is a good place for you.

Sincerely,
Catelyn

Then I got more paper and wrote more notes of apology to every kid at the school that I'd teased, including Henry, Toy, and Suzanne. By the time I was finished, I was tired and sad. I would get my dad to drop the notes off at school. Then I lay down in my bed and thought about Jason. He'd been my boyfriend for a year and I thought that I loved him. He was also a great hockey player, and we went to each other's games and talked about applying for hockey scholarships. We'd gone skating all last winter, our favorite sport, and used to do practice shots and play on his backyard rink. The thought of losing his respect just killed me. I knew that he would never have said those things to me… unless he meant them.

By the time Mom and Dad got home, I was ready to see one of the counselors that Mrs. MacDonald had recommended. I spent the remainder of my suspension going to appointments, doing homework, and reading or thinking and writing in my journal about turning over my life.

When I returned to school, it took everyone quite a while to get used to the change. I didn't hang out in the old places, where I used to fool around every day. I started going to the library to study and read, whenever I had a spare. I went home right after school. With the counselor's help, I found out more about why I was a bully and that I would need time to recover, which caused me to develop patience and tolerance and to take more time with everything I did. This wasn't easy, unlike other things which have always come easily to me in terms of school and my social life. Now I wanted to be successful in a completely new way and I was willing to do whatever it took. A lot of my friends started to hang out with other people as a result.

One day, my home form teacher gave me an envelope. I opened it up and found a note card with a kitten on the front. Inside was a message from Melissa.

Dear Catelyn,

Thank you for your apology. It helped me to recover. I can't imagine what would make you say and do the things you did to someone you hardly know, but I think that it took courage to write me and I admire that. I am feeling much better now and I hope you never do anything like that again to anyone.

Good luck,
Melissa

I realized that she didn't have to write that note and though the memory of what I did would never go away, her thoughts gave me some inspiration to do something more. When Mr. Sullivan set up a cross-cultural conflict mediation workshop the next week, I was the first student to sign up and become a leader-in-training.

Commentary

A bully who is popular is harder to spot than the blatantly hostile kids who pick on others in open and physical ways. Catelyn is clever and full of promise. She is a likeable student, full of the physical energy that many adolescents lack. As a member of a racial minority group, she has been picked on because of her skin color and desire to fit in as a member of the majority culture. Such discrimination has lasting effects, which are shown in the ways she and her friends pick on vulnerable kids who can't stand up to her. Like a lot of bullies, she doesn't identify what she's doing as bullying; she thinks that she is just fooling around. She is a powerful influence on other kids who fall under her spell, and who will support her actions actively or passively, or at the least not oppose her. It is hard to perceive the unpleasant aspects of her bright personality and teachers may not recognize the aggressive side of her nature. Because they present so winningly, such students can usually conceal a lot from adults.

The truth is that Catelyn struggles with her own vulnerability and shuts out her past, preferring to focus on the present. This is exactly why she picks on vulnerable kids; they carry the very qualities she is repressing. She really doesn't have a lot of self-knowledge and this weakness combined with her natural exuberance makes her a bully. That she can, when prodded by her parents, look at her memories of being bullied and connect them with her present actions shows the kind of strength and dignity she possesses.

In all of this, Catelyn is typical of most bullies, who pick on the vulnerable precisely because they have disowned their own emotional past and don't recognize it when they inflict it on others. Her kind of bullying is often found on athletic teams and within groups of popular kids at private and public schools..

For those working in a school environment, the best approach to take with students like Catelyn is to pay attention to their relationships with others in group settings. Teachers should not allow them to always sit with their friends; instead, pair them up with less talkative and lively students, where they have to slow down and listen and support.

Teachers can also encourage the leadership abilities of these students in positive and responsible ways. For example, in sports, these students may be encouraged to help players less powerful than themselves so that they are not only identifying with the best. In class, they can be challenged to think about many sides of a problem, not just the obvious.

All high schools should implement conflict mediation programs, which train kids to solve conflicts and become leaders. One excellent source of information for these types of program is available through St. Stephen's House (www.ststephenshouse.com/crs.shtml).

At home, parents can monitor how much socializing is done via e-mail and cell phone conversations by asking younger kids what they and their friends are writing about. Remind them that sending unkind or abusive e-mails is wrong and can land them in serious trouble. Many parents do not allow their child to be in an MSN conversation group until they are in senior public school.

In daily conversation with kids, parents need to listen *without* judgment and, afterwards, give their opinion in a thoughtful way ("Here's what I think…") or ask an older child, "Do you want to know what I think?" Take time to be alone with your child, perhaps on a special trip to visit a museum, see a game or movie, have a meal out. This provides an opportunity to listen and to hear about what is going on in their lives at home and at school. Of course, asking children to help out at home and do chores and ordinary tasks is always a good way to keep them focused on reality and involved with you.

Activities
(These activities are intended for use within a classroom setting.)
1. Pair withdrawn students with lively students and have them interview each other about their interests, likes, dislikes, favorite things, places they've traveled, pets, etc. and then have each "introduce" the other to the larger class.

2. Prepare some slips of paper, one for each person in the class. On each slip of paper, write an instruction, such as "Only speak to people wearing yellow," "If you have blue eyes you must lie down on the floor," "Give a compliment to everyone with brown eyes," "Avoid people wearing blue," "You must bow to people wearing pink," etc. Fold the papers and place them in a basket. Have each student choose a piece of paper from the basket and have them follow the instructions. Afterwards, discuss how the exercise felt and how this reflects the biases we all develop against each other. As a group, list some of the biases that students carry to school and sometimes express toward each other. Where do these biases come from?

3. Write a list of "rules" that keep us being free of prejudice in our lives.

4. Creative writing/storytelling exercise: Write and/or tell a story about a time when you learned a lesson the hard way. Choose an incident that still affects your life today.

6

Vincent

"Sometimes I wish I were dead."

When I was nine years old, my mother died and my father, who traveled a lot, thought it better for me if I lived at my nonna's, my grandmother's. So I moved into her house on Miller Street. The first night, Dominic, the boy next door, came over with *his* nonna to visit. He was a small, dark-haired kid my age, who I knew from previous visits with my nonna and nonno.

"Why are you moving in?" he asked.

"Cause my dad travels," I answered.

"Do you want to play a video game?" He swayed back and forth from one foot to the other. He was shorter than me.

"Okay."

Though Dominic was kind of bossy and always wanted to play a game he chose, he was also fun and quite smart. His nonna, whom he lived with, was best friends with mine.

"What grade will you be in?" he asked when I was leaving his house after the game.

"Five."

"Cool. Maybe we'll be in the same class," he grinned.

It was hot that summer and there wasn't a lot to do. I'd stare out the window and watch the squirrels running up and down the trees and along the telephone wires. The big dog tied up in the front yard across the street seemed sad, standing there alone for hours, wailing, "Arooooooo." I wondered why people would have a dog if they had to keep him tied up outside all day.

Now and then Dominic came over to ask me to hang out. We played videos and watched TV and horsed around on the street playing kick ball. "It's neat that you live here now. There was no one my age to play with before," he told me.

On the first day, we walked to school together. When we arrived in the schoolyard, some boys called, "Yo, Dominic!" and ran over to him. The next minute he walked off, leaving me standing alone. This happened every day. Yet, after school, we'd walk home.

The next week, during recess, Dominic came towards me with a group of boys. He nudged one called Nicky who walked up to me and said, "Hey! Loser" and "Psycho." They all laughed. I thought it was a joke until I saw Dominic's face, twisted and sneering, as he laughed at what the boy had said. I mumbled, "No I'm not, I am not!" I walked away from them to the doors of the school, my face burning.

Later that week, he got his friends to gang up because, "Vincent isn't athletic. Vincent is a pansy."

I told my teacher, "Some boys are picking on me at recess."
"Who?"
"Dominic and his friends: Nicky and Michael and others."

She called them over to her desk. "Dominic, Michael, Nicky, you know the rules, 'No bullying and fighting at school under any conditions.'" The boys acted surprised that I had told her. Dominic shrugged, "We were just horsing around. We didn't mean any harm to Vincent."

She looked at them over her glasses, "Don't play rough! If I hear this again, you'll all go to the office. Now sit down."

The next time they waited for me off school property.

Every morning, Dominic waited till I came out, and then he'd call, "Hey, Vince!" He'd walk towards me even if I kept on walking, but as soon as his friends came into sight, he'd move on and start fooling with them. One day, he murmured something and they started chanting, "Vincie's a gay boy." Another day they called out, "Stupid over there, he has to tell the teacher."

At school, although they were careful, they sometimes bumped or tripped me, pushed me against the wall, and shouted, "Hey, look out!" as if it were an accident. That afternoon, the gym teacher said, "Vince, go and wash your face," and in the mirror I saw blood running down the side of my face from where I had scraped it on the wall. I thought it odd that this teacher, Mr. DaCosta, had been on yard duty and had actually seen them push me. But he'd just turned around and walked away.

Sometimes they followed me at a distance and someone would yell, "Tackle him!" and one at a time, they jumped on top of me, pretending that this was a football play and I was the ball. I'd lie at the bottom with their heavy, stinky bodies falling on top of me, holding my hands over my head for protection. They'd laugh so hard I could feel their bodies shaking on me. Such a big joke! After they'd left, I'd turn over and look up at the sky and wonder what I did to Dominic to deserve this. I'd stand up and brush myself off and go home. When I came in, Nonna always asked, "How your day go?" and I always answered, "It was okay."

I liked watching TV after school. My favorite show, which I used to watch with my mom, was *Jerry Springer*. One day, his guests were a heavy woman with long blonde hair and her best friend who lived beside her. The blonde woman told Jerry, "…and she tells lies about me, and steals my mail, and borrows my things and never returns them…" Her best friend, black-haired, wearing red cowboy boots, was shaking her head, mouthing, "No, no, no." The audience, hooting and hollering, seemed to take the side of the dark-haired one until she shouted worse things at her blonde friend.

I was afraid of fighting. I detested the sight of blood; it made me squirm, though whenever I imagined taking revenge, I saw myself firing at Dominic and his friends with a machine gun; blood, bones, and guts flying everywhere. There I'd be, covered in it in the middle of the battle, and even when the police arrived, I'd be in charge. I wouldn't run away.

Dominic probably guessed how scared I was. He knew I'd never fight back and that I'd never tell anyone at home. How many times had I heard my nonno say, "Italians don't take sh-- from nobody." After school, there he'd be, sleeping on the couch after his shift. Even though he was over 50, his thick muscles bulged out of his T-shirt. He was in good shape for an old man. If he thought that I was being beaten up and not doing anything about it, he'd never let me forget it.

Whenever I said to Nonna, "Can I stay home tomorrow? I don't feel good," my nonno barked, "Hey, you're not going to let an ache stop you! No way! I get up at 4 a.m. every morning and go to work when everyone else is sleeping. Work all day. Never taken a day off, no matter what. I just go to bed early. That's what you should do."

If he knew that I was letting these boys get away with this, he'd have a cow.

My nonna usually let me stay home.

I tried to protect myself. I'd walk to and from school after all the other kids had left, but they seemed to have mental telepathy and be waiting for me on the street corner, "Hey, here comes Stupid."

At home, Dominic pretended that it never happened, or that it was all a big joke. Every weekend he asked me to play some game or video like we were best friends. One Saturday we were playing at his house, I asked, "Why do you and your friends treat me so mean at school?" He shrugged, "Oh, we're just kidding. It doesn't mean anything." He had this dumb smile on his face. I knew that I wasn't imagining this. I wondered if he was jealous because I was so much bigger than him. Guys called him nicknames like "Elf" and "Mouse." I wanted to say, "I hate going to that school because of you and your friends." I didn't, because I wanted him to think that I didn't care, that I was tough, that I was cool.

One night at supper, Nonna stared at my neck. "Where did you get that purple bruise?" she asked. I kept eating. She looked at Nonno. "Do you see those bruises?" Nonno said, "What were you doing?" I finally spoke, "Uh, it's nothing, some boys jumped me." Nonna asked, "Why? What did you do?"

"Nothing!" I took my dishes to the sink and went upstairs. But when my dad came over later that night, Nonna told him about the bruises and my dad looked came up to look. "That's a nasty bruise, Vince. What made the boys do this?"

I shrugged in my pajamas. "I don't know why, but Dominic and his friends play this game where they jump on me like football tackle."

"Are they joking?"

"Maybe, I don't know, uh, I don't think so. I don't want to talk about it."

"Do you want me to speak to the school about it?"

"No, I don't want it to get worse."

"Yeah, but you don't have to take this."

"They won't stop."

The next day, my dad called the school and complained to the principal, who said he'd investigate. When he called my dad back, he said that the boys, who were all good students and on the school hockey team, claimed that I was making it all up and they were just playing around. The principal added, "Maybe Vince needs more attention from home."

My dad promised, "I'll get those kids myself; they won't try this again!" but he never did. They were never around when he was home and out looking for them. When he spoke to Dominic's nonna, she said that Dominic insisted that I was doing this to him. My dad asked me, "Look, do you have your story right? Are you certain these boys were targeting you?"

"Of course," I choked, almost crying. Did he think I made it up? It seemed hopeless if my dad didn't understand.

"Don't let it get you down. Summer's almost here," he said, and took me to have pizza and to see a movie.

That night, I lay in bed fantasizing that I was flying up to the top of the ceiling and out the window, rising higher and higher, above the clouds and stars, up into the great dark sky to meet... my mom?

In Grade 6, on the way home from school, Nicky said, "Your mom was a drug addict wasn't she?" The other boys chanted, "His mom was a druggie, that's why he's so dumb!" I went ballistic, turned around and ran at them with my fists clenched and stopped just before their noses. I shouted, "You better shut up or I'll kill you all!" They ran away, leaving me there on the sidewalk.

The next morning at school, they went to the office and told the principal that I threatened to kill them. Without knowing this, I was called to the principal's office and they phoned my home.

Our principal, Mr. Martini, was a younger, athletic guy who sometimes wore sneakers with his tie and jacket. He asked me into his office. "This is a pretty serious threat. Why did you tell those boys that you would kill them?"

"Umm... Dominic's spreading stories about my mom."

"What kind of stories?" asked Mr. Martini. "It's important that I hear these things."

"He said that my mom was a drug addict."

"Your mom passed away, didn't she?"

I nodded.

"So you feel protective about your mother... Yes, well, I understand that you don't like Dominic making fun of your mom, but to say that you're going to kill him is not a good way to handle it. You could get into serious trouble for threatening someone."

"I didn't mean that I was going to do it."

"Words are stronger than you think, Vincent. Even if someone makes you very angry, you have to control yourself. Count to 50 and then you won't feel so angry. That's what I do. Do you understand me?"

"Yes, sir. But what about Dominic? Him and his friends on the hockey team always pick on me."

"Well, I will speak with them again. We can't have this kind of behavior in our school."

He smiled.

I left his office and went back to class.

My nonna was excited when I got home. As she salted the eggplant, she asked, "What happened? Eh? Why the school call me? What you do?" My grandfather was angry. "Why does the school call us? What trouble did you do?"

"Dom said some things..." I began.

"What he say?" Nonno demanded.

I cried and told them what the boys had shouted.

Nonno shook his head. "You stand up to them; you let them know that they can't get away with this." Nonna said, "Dominic heard that from his nonna. That's the only place he would hear that."

She dropped her work and went to the phone and called Dom's grandmother to tell her about what happened. But his nonna was insulted and started yelling at my nonna: "Vincent always lies and starts trouble." My nonna yelled back, "Dom is a bully to my Vincent." My nonna was saying, "I believe Vincent" when her friend hung up the phone.

That's how they stopped speaking for a year, because Dom said that I was a liar.

I talked to my aunt Franca about it. She was a teacher and had her own class. "I never pick on other kids," I said. "Why do they pick on me and anyone else who isn't like them?"

"Maybe they're insecure…" she said, "maybe they're jealous."

"But I accept that everyone is different. It would be boring if we were all the same."

She said, "That's right. It's not okay that these kids are getting away with this."

"Do you have kids like me at your school?" I asked. She smiled.

"Sure, but we don't let other kids pick on them repeatedly like what's happening to you."

The next afternoon, she dropped by after school to see my principal.

When she came home, she called me up to her room. "Well, I'm not impressed with Mr. Martini. When I told him why I came, and about your bruises and the nonsense going on with these kids since Grade 5, he said, 'There's no serious problem here. Boys will be boys. One minute they're fighting, the next they're laughing.' Then he said, 'Vince needs to lighten up and have some fun participating instead of being a loner all the time. All the teachers say that Vince needs to get involved.' He couldn't care less, that one," she added. "What are you going to do?"

"Nothing," I answered. "What can I do?"

She hugged me. "Well, I'll help you with any schoolwork, so don't let this get you down."

I nodded. I knew she was trying to help me.

By Grade 7, I found a way of blocking out these kids, by keeping my head down and by minding my own business. In class, I always sat at the back and kept my eyes down. I never answered any questions or stood out in any way. Outside I stayed by the fence and ignored everyone till the bell rang. After school, I hurried out ahead of everyone and got home before anything happened. I kept my nose clean, hurried home right after school to play on my computer or watch TV. I started smoking when nobody was home.

Nonno didn't like to see me sitting around, didn't want me smoking. He was tired and irritable from labor.

"Hey you, deadbeat," he said. "Get off your butt! You sack of potatoes, all you do is sit and watch TV. Back in Italy I never went to school. I never had your chances to learn and play. I had to go to work in the fields when I was five years old!" He'd grab the remote from me and stop me from watching my shows so he could see his Italian shows, which I hated.

It became a game, a way of letting off steam for us. Swearing at each other, punching and shoving each other on the couch, doing nasty things like me hiding the remote or his whiskey that he always sipped in the afternoon while he watched his news, or him hiding my cola or potato chips. We insulted each other. "Old man," I'd snarl, and he called me "b-----d" and "retard."

This was our daily workout – to sit and insult each other in the worst ways we could imagine. "No girl will ever love you, fat slob," he'd say, and I'd say, "Old man, drop dead, no one will miss you." My nonna would hear us and shout, "Stop fighting," and my dad and my aunt tried to make us be peaceful, so we whispered our insults and swears so no one would stop us – "lazy pig" and "old snot." It was funny, in a way, compared to school.

The summer before high school was the worst of my life. That was because Dom spent the summer watching me with a pair of binoculars. Every time I went outside, he'd come out and watch me. I always liked to help my nonno plant and weed in his garden, but now I hated being there. If I even came out on my verandah, he'd suddenly appear, watching me through these little black glasses. The same if I came out the back door. It was driving me crazy. I shouted, "Leave me alone, Dominic. Don't be such an a--h---," but he just grinned and went on watching me through the binoculars. I stopped going outside. By summer's end, my skin was as white as a ghost.

In Grade 9, I thought that I was getting away from him, but at the last moment Dominic and I ended up going to the same school. The first day that he saw me in the hall he shouted, "There he is, my psycho neighbor," and at lunch I overheard him say, "He's so gay."

I was now much taller than him, yet I still couldn't just plow him one, even though I knew that I had a right. I avoided him as much as possible.

My aunt Franca encouraged me with girls: "You are a hunk!"

"Get real," I said, "I am not.

"Vince, you're tall, your bones are great, you are good-looking. Watch out for the girls." She laughed and gave me a hug.

But I began to see it, when I looked in the mirror. I saw the same face and body, yet with more angles, and more filled out in my shoulders. I asked my dad for some new clothes and every morning I'd spend a longer time with my grooming. It paid off.

There were two cute girls in my class, Mona and Arietta, who talked to me at lunch in the cafeteria. The problem was that I couldn't think of anything to say to them. I just kept smiling. Every day, I'd think of things to say to them, but when I was with them, I got tongue-tied.

Soon Dominic noticed and he and his friends started talking to these girls, too. When I joined them, they'd say, "Here he comes, Miss America," and everyone laughed.

I walked away and never went near these girls again. Any time Dominic passed me in the hall or anywhere, he'd make these girlish gestures and his friends called out in falsettos, "Oh, Vincie, are you going dancing with him tonight?" They spread stories around that I was a misfit and couldn't play sports.

I was afraid to go to school in case I might do something to one of these goofs. When I heard them calling out insults, I started shaking and imagined myself smashing them with a hammer over the head. I could see the guy falling back into the lockers, his head cut open, blood oozing down his face. Now I couldn't concentrate on my homework, and I found it hard to study for term tests. I smoked more, despite my nonno's house rules, and my marks dropped 20 percent.

Aunt Franca said, "I'll help you with your homework." Together we sat at the kitchen table in the evening, me doing homework while she did lesson preps and marked assignments. If I had a project due, she'd help me to complete it. While we were making a collage about Greek myths for English class, I told her about the guys at school. "I'm afraid," I confided, "I'm so angry."

"You've got to tell the guidance office," she urged.

But when I got an appointment with my guidance officer, Mrs. Filakowski, she asked, "What's wrong? Your marks are sliding downwards."

"This boy from my other school is spreading stuff about me."

"Such as?"

"That I'm gay and retarded and other stuff."

She shook her head and read over my school record. There were posters on her walls, one for college showed students laughing over their books as if they'd won the jackpot. Another poster showed a student over a telephone, his head bent in obvious distress. The caption read, "You're not alone. Let someone help." Underneath was the Distress Center call number. She looked up at me, "You certainly are bright enough, above average. And it appears as if this isn't the first time you've had some trouble with other kids calling you names," she said.

"No, and it's always been Dominic. He turns kids against me."

She looked up at me. "Well, you are big and you are smart. Can't you tell them to stop?"

I stared at her in amazement. Didn't she know what was going on in the high school? Obviously not. "Um, they don't listen to me. I've tried. They just keep on, day after day. That's one reason why I'm absent a lot."

She made some notes and said, "We have to work on this problem together, Vincent. You have to stand up to these guys and show them that you're not going to take it and I will speak to Dominic and some of your teachers so that they know what's going on." Maybe she did, but I never made another appointment with her again.

Nothing changed that year that I could notice. Dominic didn't call me anything, in fact we didn't speak, but that didn't matter because the damage was done. Kids I didn't know shoved and pushed me around, and called me names. I told myself that I wouldn't fight them no matter what, because I knew that if I did, I'd kill them I was so mad.

The next three years passed in a blur. By autumn of Grade 12, my nerves were shot. I'd gained a ton of weight from eating junk food, my hands shook, and I smoked a pack or more a day just to calm down.

Hardly anyone spoke to me at school now, since the previous year I'd jumped up and exploded at these morons one day in class, "LEAVE ME ALONE AND GET THE F   OUTTA MY FACE!!"

The office sent me home that day to rest, and after that, kids were afraid of me; they thought I was scary. If I met Dominic, he'd cross to the other side of the street or the hall. Good, I felt that I had won. He was now afraid of me.

Aunt Franca would say, "Vince, let's read, let's do some math." We'd sit at the table and do homework, but she was worried. I wouldn't tell her or my father anything.

She visited the school on parents' night in October and spoke to the guidance counselor and the vice principal. The vice principal said, "Vince is his own worst enemy. He doesn't get involved, he plays the victim. He's anti social, he never smiles."

My aunt told the guidance counselor about my depression. The counselor said, "There are over 1000 students in this school and we are doing our best for Vince, and there is no bullying allowed in this school."

My aunt came back and said, "They couldn't care less about a kid like you."

Then in December it all fell in on me. I couldn't go to school anymore. I couldn't get up out of bed till afternoon. I didn't have any energy, except to smoke and drink coffee and watch the cartoon channel or play on the computer my dad bought me.

When I did go, I fell asleep in class because I couldn't concentrate on anything the teachers were saying.

I just wanted to die, to go far away and never return. A deadness had descended over my mind like the black curtains on the school auditorium stage.

My family was worried about me. Even Nonno stopped calling me names and Nonna prayed for me in her rosary group. My dad took me out for dinners, bought me clothes and cigarettes, but nothing worked. My closest friend was a cigarette. I only felt happy when I was smoking. Dragging in the smoke tasted good and filled me up, made me less edgy. I lit one cigarette off another. I wasn't angry; I didn't feel anything. It was my aunt Franca who got me to see the family doctor. He recommended a psychiatrist who specialized in teenagers.

At first I didn't want to go and refused to keep the appointment. "No, I don't wanna talk to some shrink. People will think I'm psycho."

"You'll just talk about yourself a bit. This doctor will be like a friend."

"I don't need friends."

My aunt spoke to Nonno. That night when I was lying on the couch smoking he said, "Hey, if you sick, you need a doctor, eh? If your leg a broke you see a doctor to get it set, right? So, it's the same; you see the doctor if you don't feel good inside."

I stared at him. I couldn't believe this old man was telling me to see a head doctor. Was I dreaming?

"Come on, your family love you and want you to get help." He stood there by the TV almost pleading with me.

The next week my dad drove me to the hospital where this doctor had an office. He promised that no one would know outside of the family.

Dr. Jamison wore jeans and a jacket – not what I expected. I found it hard to look at her at first, but she didn't care when I only stared at the carpet.

I started to see her twice a week. Sometimes we sat in silence. "You don't have to speak if you don't want to."

She put me on medication for depression and said, "You ignored and fought the bullies at school, but you identified with them inside yourself. You need to start all over again." In the spring I started night school for a Grade 12 course. It was hard to concentrate, but my aunt Franca helped me and everyone in the family encouraged me: "You can do this, Vince."

I began to remember when I lived with my mom and my dad and I told the doctor memories about them and my nonna and nonno. After a year, I began to feel anger at Dominic, but I also saw over the weeks and months and year how much I had been living inside myself and had no energy to stand up to him. Dr. Jamison said that I was "unable to fight back because you've never recovered from losing your mom," and she compared my grief to my being put under a terrible spell like Beast in the old fairy tale *Beauty and the Beast*.

I was still ashamed that I had to see a shrink and take pills and drop out of school. Sometimes I'd see Dominic passing my house on the way to catch the bus for university. Even though I was now behind him in school, maybe it was better because I was taking control. I didn't snap so much at Nonno and I'd cut back to a pack of cigarettes.

I was taking more night courses and thinking about university. Dr. Jamison got me writing a journal, for my dreams and thoughts. As I wrote in it, I realized that I had been so sad for so long. I remembered the principal telling my aunt that I never smiled at anyone. Now I knew why.

Commentary

Vince is an introvert and an isolate. As such, he's the kind of kid many parents and teachers find difficult to understand – a situation that is made worse by the fact that, like most children, Vince is unable to tell the adults in his life how he is struggling both inside and outside the home. Vince is also typical of immigrant children, who often grow up without parents in the country and/or are raised by an older generation that does not speak English and that cannot represent the child at school. Vince is very much on his own as a result of losing his mother, living with much older grandparents, and not being able to communicate well with his own father. From this place of isolation, he is unable to defend himself against his neighbor, who takes advantage of his vulnerable situation. Vince's story could have been much more tragic. Many children like him become so angry that they either do something violent to the offenders or to themselves.

Teachers find a student like Vince difficult to assist, because he doesn't really make any trouble in class, and because he is also unable to communicate anything of what he is about. A teacher, therefore, has to be vigilant in reading the body language of all the kids, taking time to draw out those who don't readily present themselves, and using class lessons in history, literature, science, and health to appeal to seemingly passive and uninterested kids by including details and images that help to draw them out.

All subject areas present an opportunity to use Top Dog/Underdog analogies, which point out that there is always a balance of power in nature and in human society, and that while people need to protect themselves, they must also help to defend others who may be weaker and need their support. Usually, bullies have friends who support them, giving them an unfair advantage over their victims. Top Dog/Underdog strategies help kids to think about power and responsibility, and to start recognizing the balance of power in any situation in class, on the schoolyard, or at home. They can start thinking about how they can help someone who is in an underdog situation and needs assistance to set the balance right. By referring Top Dog/Underdog analogies and strategies, teachers assist students to connect their own experience with every part of life and learning.

A parent has to win the trust of this kind of child by being "present," in terms of listening to what they say, not making a lot of judgments, supporting their choices, and spending "down time" with them. To do this, the parent may have to reorganize their own life, perhaps making more time for being with the family. A quiet child like Vincent tests everyone's patience and imagination, for they ask that you walk in their shoes and understand their experience.

Activities and questions for discussion
(For adults and youths)

1. Create skits or imagine the balance of power between two people in the following five places. If the balance is weighted too heavily and unfairly in one direction, where one person is Top Dog to another's Underdog, correct it. You can also do this exercise by using role playing in groups; it's a great way to practice changing the balance of power in a situation.
   a) restaurant
   b) school
   c) church
   d) playground/park
   e) home/work

2. Who do you identify with in this story: Vincent or Dominic? Describe how such situations happen in your own life. Is there something that you would like to change? List the ways that you can do that.

3. Write a letter to a friend or a relative telling them why you like them, and what would make you more relaxed and trusting with them. What have you learned about yourself and the way you communicate with others?

4. Is there any person in your community that you perceive as an isolate or loner? How could you connect with them?

7

Lauren

"I was shunned by the whole school."

That first day back to high school in senior year seemed normal enough. I'd been away most of the summer working at camp and hadn't seen lots of people since June. The halls were full of students milling about, shouting out greetings, crowding around the class schedules taped to the walls, hurrying to the office to pick up their timetables.

Most of the seniors were kids I knew from earlier years, so we all had lots to talk about. All the juicy stuff like who got together with who, or broke up with who, who did what with who, who had a new boy/girlfriend, summer romances, summer bashes when the parents were away…

Jeff had just come back too; he'd been at his parents' cottage so we had to catch up. His sun bleached hair was long, as if he'd just driven back from a long summer snooze. He looked "down." I knew from his letters he'd been missing me a lot, smoking a lot of weed, and having anxiety attacks. He'd had to take some meds for that and was hoping to get good marks so he could get into a top university.

Most of us were talking about that, it being our last year, and the pressure to get those marks. I was hoping for a scholarship, knowing that my parents couldn't afford anything like Jeff's could. Morgan came up to my locker with his arm around his new squeeze, a chick in Grade 11 who was supposed to be "sexy." He dropped her hand and picked me up and swung me around! I screamed and laughed for the first time in weeks. Morgan was my best friend, closer than anybody other than Jeff, and we hadn't spoken since a wild party at his parents' cottage last June. More and more seniors swarmed around us, jostling each other. We all hung out in a big group and we pretty well ran the school – the student council, the football team, the music, art and drama clubs.

In the office, I ran into Eva, and Kevin, her steady boyfriend, as we picked up our individual timetables. We squealed when we saw each other; we'd been best friends from Grade 5. We scanned our timetables: "Hey, we're in the same section of biology and art. Great!" We groaned about some of the teachers we got and went off to join the long lineup at the guidance office, to switch to a better time or class. Morgan was there and Jeff, too, and we rejoiced that we were all in the same biology class with Mr. Miller. It was amazing, all of us together again for one last great year.

Afterwards, we all went to KFC for a Toonie Tuesday lunch. We went to the park across the street and over little boxes of greasy chicken we talked about our summers. Morgan had had a great summer as a swimming instructor at a camp in Algonquin. Eva had worked in the city at a "Stitches" jeans shop. She had no tan, but Kevin looked dark enough from working on a cousin's farm driving the tractor all summer. Jeff had gone first to the camp he's attended since he was eight, then spent the rest of the summer at his parents' island cottage in the north. I told them about the Guide camp where I'd been the "Tripping Counselor" and taken senior campers on canoe trips through a wilderness park. We'd survived it all – black flies, thunderstorms, stomach flu. I'd come back to the city appreciating the luxuries of hot showers and coffee lattes.

When I got up to go home, Jeff said he'd call me later and I found myself walking with Morgan. He wanted to know if anything hot had happened after I got home from camp. Had I gone to many clubs? Had I had any good drugs? Morgan was a real druggie, something that he concealed from the staff advisors he worked with as sports editor of the school newspaper and yearbook. We always talked about drugs and their effect on us. I trusted him as much as Jeff, maybe more, or I wouldn't have told him about it.

He was also good at weaseling the dirt out of anyone. "Come on," he'd say, "tell me about it."

I told him things I'd never tell Kevin or Eva, knowing that she didn't approve of drugs, with her coming from such an addicted family as hers was. "Do you promise to keep your lid on this?" I asked him.

"Who am I going to tell?" he asked.

"Your new squeeze, whatshername, for starters."

"It's Krista, and I wouldn't tell her! She's a babe in the woods about a lot of things I do. Also, she has a rather strict feminist mother."

"Well, I don't want you to tell anyone this. I haven't even told Jeff and I don't want to."

Morgan shivered and showed his dimples. "Ooo, this sounds juicy. I won't breathe a word of it."

We stopped by a panhandler who put his hand put in front of us. "Spare some change kids?"

I reached into my bag and found a loonie. "Here you go."

"God bless." He was probably younger than he looked, like most of the panhandlers who hung around the downtown.

Morgan shook his head. "I wouldn't waste my money on those losers. He could work if he wanted. You're promoting him by giving him money, you know." A frown creased his handsome face.

I shrugged. "I don't care. I like to help those guys. It could be me or even you some day."

Morgan shrieked. "Oh yeah, you're just an old bleeding heart, Lauren." He smiled wide. "Anyway, what went down? In the summer? I want to hear the good stuff."

"Okay, I went to a club with a few friends in August, when I got back. I didn't know anyone there. And I really took more drugs as the night wore on, more than I should have, and I forgot to drink water, so by 4 a.m. I was so wasted I could hardly stand up. And these guys that I'd been hanging with asked if they could help me out and I went with them because they at least could stand up and I wanted to lie down."

I stopped for breath and Morgan said, "Did you know them? Don't stop now."

"Just a minute. I didn't know them, though one's name was John and another was Troy. Well, we went to this guy's house and down to this rec room or something, and the next thing I know I was on the floor and I think these guys were taking down their pants and well, they...

they *all* did it with me, I think. I can't remember. I couldn't have stopped it if I tried and I didn't. I was wasted like I said. I slept it off at his place and stumbled home around noon the next day."

Morgan was silent and then he spoke. "Wow! What an afterparty! How are you feeling now? Have you seen those guys since?"

"No," I said, "And I don't ever want to. I'm sorry now that it happened. It was dumb, I guess."

"Oh, well, you were having a good time; I hope it was a good time."

"I can't quite remember, it's all a blur." We were at my street so we stood talking a bit longer. "Well, see you tomorrow. Remember to keep it under your hat."

"Don't worry," he said, "I've forgotten it already. See you tomorrow!"

I didn't speak to anyone else about it, not even to the girls I went with to the club that night. I didn't tell Jeff, of course, because he'd be hurt.

The weeks of school followed each other as always, and everything seemed great. I settled down to my homework every night and only fooled around on the weekends when it was all done. I wasn't going to let anything screw up my chances for a scholarship.

Jeff was fooling around, though, smoking up and skipping like he didn't care. We talked on the phone every night and he was usually high.

A couple of days later, Eva and I talked in our spare about Jeff. She said she didn't like his drug use. "I think people who have to get high with drugs are weak! I really do."

I said nothing.

She continued, "My cousin Jake smokes up every day and has no ambition whatsoever. He just wants to sit around and go to this little job at Starbucks and that's it! He's pathetic!"

"Jeff can't communicate at home," I said. "His dad is really stiff and stuff, a big cheese. They can't talk."

"That's no excuse," Eva sniffed.

"Yeah, I agree." I had problems, too. My mom was sometimes in and out of the psychiatric ward and I had to look after the younger kids and cook for my dad.

We all had problems it seemed, even Morgan, whose parents were fun alcoholics; he had to help them into bed at night on the weekend after their parties.

"At least we have goals and we're productive," Eva whispered.

I submitted my assignments and got A's on everything. As October started, it looked like I was going to score a 90 percent midterm report. I was happier than I'd been in months and Jeff and I went to sit in the park and feed the birds some peanuts I had brought from home. He was failing, he told me. "How come?" I asked. "Don't you care about university?"

He threw some peanuts to a big fat pigeon. "Of course, but I just can't study, no motivation. I dunno. I just can't put my mind on anything."

"I could help you," I offered.

"Nah, it's okay. I'll try harder. But let's smoke some new weed I got."

He was immature, that's what, but the sweetest guy in the school. In the back of my mind I worried that if he didn't get with it, I might lose interest, or at least we'd lose some of the things we had in common. When the bag was empty, we went over to his house to hang out and to get something to eat.

It was the second week in October and I walked into the biology class and threw my backpack on the floor by my desk. "Hey," I said to Eva, who was sitting in the next desk. She was talking to Kevin. "Eva?" I thought she hadn't heard me.

She didn't turn back until Mr. Miller walked into the class, and didn't catch my eye or turn towards me once in the class. I had the distinct feeling that she was ignoring me on purpose. I turned and asked another friend, Rose Ann, for a lab sheet. She shook her head like she was listening and didn't want to be bothered. I glanced over at Kevin and he looked away. What was going on? What was this big freeze?

Morgan came up after class. "How's it goin'?" he asked. "Everyone's acting weird," I said as Jeff came up. We moved into the hall.

"Whadya mean?" Morgan asked.

I shrugged and nodded at Eva and Kevin, who just walked past us without looking at me. "What's with them?" I asked.

"I dunno. See ya!" Morgan hurried off to his next class on the fourth floor.

That's how it went all day; every senior I knew seemed to avoid me, hurry past, or look the other way. No one spoke to me except Jeff and Morgan. I had the weirdest feeling of isolation. What was going on?

I hurried home after school. My mom had been acting strange again, staying home from work, looking pale, not able to sleep without pills. I prepared dinner for everyone so there'd be something to eat. As I chopped the veggies for a spaghetti sauce, I thought about the kids at school, especially Kevin and Eva. Why did she completely avoid me in our spare period? Why did she and Kevin hurry past me at the end of the day? I felt excluded, as if they knew something about me that I didn't know. I decided to wait and see, usually the best policy. No sense getting your "knickers in a knot," as my dad put it.

But the next day and the rest of the week were the same, and even worse, as more and more students seemed to give me chilly glances as they passed me in the hall. I told Jeff about it, but he knew nothing. Morgan was still friendly, pausing to stop and joke in the morning. Most seniors were freaking out about next week's midterms.

On Friday, I stopped at Eva's locker and said, "Can I speak to you for a minute, Eva?"

Kevin heard me. His face pink, he said, "Uh, look, Lauren, I don't know how to say this, but, uh, Eva doesn't want to talk to you, and I don't either. We heard what you did at a party in the summer and well… you should be ashamed of what you did. You proved that you are… a… a skank. Like, I'm being blunt. We don't want to hang with you."

My face was straight, though I flushed as I always do when I'm embarrassed.

Eva turned to him. "Let's get to class." And they walked away, leaving me there stunned.

When I turned around, I saw Morgan and Krista. "Hey Lauren!" he called. I walked towards him, my heart pounding hard, my lips dry. "Hey, what's the matter?" he asked.

"How many people did you tell about me, Morgan?" I said. "Are you going to publish it in the school paper?"

His face grew pale and for the first time since I knew him, he was speechless. He recovered himself then, and spluttered, "Hey, wait a minute... I told one person, Kevin, okay? He blabbed it around. Blame him if you want. Mr. Morality there doesn't think you're clean enough for his standards."

"You betrayed me, Morgan. I told you not to tell *anyone*. I don't care about Kevin's judgments. I care that you didn't care enough about me and told him!"

His face was like a mask. "Oh, I am sorry, Lauren..." but I turned and walked away.

I hurried out of the school with my eyes to the ground, but after a few blocks I slowed and then stopped to sit in the park.

The pigeons came pecking around to see what I had for them. "Not today, fellows," I said. I watched two panhandlers sharing a bottle on another bench nearby.

So that's what this was all about. Betrayal and judgment. I knew that Kevin could be very strong in his beliefs. He had told the art teacher, Ms. Murdoch, where to go last year, when she'd criticized his project, which was these rubber chickens all squeezed in a wire coop sculpture, with an artistic statement about animals being used for human consumption. The teacher said it was "too obvious."

Kevin, who'd been a vegetarian for three years and who got Eva to be one too, blew his top and asked her, "What do you know about art or anything? Who are you to judge anyone's work??"

She'd taken a week's absence after that scene, she was so upset. Kevin later had to apologize and he passed.

So Kevin thinks I'm a tramp. Fine, I won't go back to school. I knew it was a wild and crazy decision, but I couldn't return to that school if everyone was shunning me like the unwed mother in *The Scarlet Letter*, which I read last year in enriched English. What was her name? Oh, yes, Hester Prynne.

I went home and threw my backpack in my closet and lay down on my bed. I could see all my studies flying out the window. I wouldn't be going to college, not next year, or the year after that. I saw all my papers, assignments flying through the air, scattering in four directions. It was too good to be true, going away to study in another city, or anywhere. We could never afford it and I didn't want to go into heavy debt that I'd never pay off.

I could get a job and work a few years and then maybe go back. I just knew one thing – I would never darken the door of the high school again.

I never told my parents what had happened to me; I just said I didn't want to go to school. Though they cried and yelled and screamed at me, I ignored them. Everything was a blur. I was so depressed. I slept in every day, I didn't eat, I sat and stared out the window. For three weeks, I was a zombie. I thought of 50 ways to kill myself, but couldn't find the energy to do anything. My mom thought I was having a breakdown and wanted me to take antidepressants, but I refused.

I didn't want to talk to anyone, though Jeff kept phoning. I finally went and met him at a coffee shop. We sat in silence for about an hour. Then I told him what was going on at school. He already knew about it and said, "It doesn't change how I feel towards you one iota. So you made a mistake. It could happen to anyone. Forget about those kids; they're not your real friends, are they?"

I lifted the foam off the top of my second latte with my finger and licked it off. "I can't believe how weak these people are. Just because Kevin makes a judgment, everyone shuns me?"

Jeff said, "Eva told me to tell you that she's sorry she can't see you, but Kevin doesn't want her to."

"What about Morgan? What's he say?"

"Oh, he's such a gossiper, he always acts so cool, but he's as bad as Kevin, spreading stuff about what girls are putting out when he does the same things himself. He cheats on Krista. He sees Mavis on Friday night and Krista on Saturday, but she doesn't know. That's pathetic, if you ask me." He leaned across the table and took my hand in his.

"How are your tests going?" I asked.

"Okay I guess; I'm passing. Teachers are all asking where you are and why you aren't turning up for tests. They have marked assignments for you."

"I don't want them."

"Nobody tells them anything. Nobody wants to talk about it."

"Good," I said.

I hadn't been at school for a month. The school called and I told the secretary that I was sick, I might have mono, and that my mom wasn't well and I wouldn't be coming back. The woman on the phone said goodbye and that was it.

The next day, Mr. Miller phoned. "Why haven't you been coming to class, Lauren? You're one of the best students and you're getting way behind."

Silence. I didn't know what to say. "Uh, gee, Mr. Miller, I'm not returning."

"Why not?"

Silence.

"Did something happen?"

Silence.

I didn't want to tell my teacher. That would be the worst humiliation, especially one of the most respected teachers in the school, who was retiring the next year.

"Lauren?"

"Yes, I'm here."

"I… wonder if we could talk in person. There's a scholarship for Life Science that I think you could get and…"

"I'm not going to university."

"Lauren, that's ridiculous. You're a fine science, well… an all-round student. Would you meet me and talk to me before you make such a crucial decision?"

"Okay."

"Where do you want to meet?"

"Uh, Starbucks?"

"Two blocks east of the school?"

"Yes."

"I have a free period tomorrow at 1:40."

"Okay"

"You'll be there then?"

"Yes, sir."

The next day, I almost slept in and missed my appointment with him, but I arrived there before he did. I was totally weirded out by meeting my teacher in Starbucks. Nobody was in there that I knew, which was a relief. Five minutes later, Mr. Miller came in, his tweed cap in his hand, and looked around. He waved at me, ordered a coffee, then sat down with the coffee in his hand.

"Hello, Lauren."

"Hi, sir."

"Well, I'm having a hard time tracking you down. I've heard everything, that you had mono, that you got a job, that you were going away, but nobody knows why you would suddenly, in the middle of first term in your senior year, leave school."

I looked at the floor.

"Can you tell me what's going on?"

I shook my head. My face was burning. What could I say? He was sipping his coffee, waiting for an answer.

"Uh, I don't know."

"What? You mean to say you don't know why you decided to quit?"

I shrugged.

"Is someone in your family sick? Are *you* sick?"

I shook my head. I felt about five years old.

"Did something happen at school?"

I nodded.

"Do you want to tell me what?"

"Some kids are spreading stuff about me and they've decided to shun me."

"*Shun* you?" He said the word as if it were an ancient concept or artifact. "Why would they do that?"

I looked at the floor and didn't answer.

"Did you do something that made them shun you?"

I nodded slightly.

"Did this happen at our school?"

I shook my head.

"Did it happen somewhere else and you told someone at school?"

"Yes."

"And they told the others."

"Yes."

"May I ask who this was?"

I shook my head.

Mr. Miller said, "You know, Lauren, I may be old and ready for pasture, but I *do* know a thing or two after teaching teenagers for 30 some years. I can see that you are suffering terribly about this shunning and have paid the price for whatever sin they're punishing you for. But you can't be too hard on yourself. You're a lovely, intelligent young woman who perhaps made an error, as we all do when we're young. You need to forgive yourself and move on. Dropping out of school is not a right response. You need to finish your year and get a scholarship and I've brought along these papers to show you all the details. It's a biology prize." He pulled the papers out of a folder he had laid on the table.

"I'm not going back there," I said quietly. I felt sorry for him, for his eagerness to inspire me.

"Now, maybe you don't want to return to this school, but you must go somewhere and graduate. It would be a crime if you didn't."

"I might go to night school."

"You need to attend day school to get your year. I urge you to reconsider this. You're someone I was certain would be near the top of the class."

"Thank you, sir."

He got up to return to the school. As he replaced his hat, he said, "Who was it that did this?"

I shook my head.

"Was it your friend Morgan? Or Kevin? Young men can be so stupid…"

I didn't answer and he left shaking his head. I phoned Jeff to join me there after school. He came in looking happy.

"Hey, howzit going?"

"Great, I guess. Oh, I've decided to go back to school."

"Here?"

"No, I think I might go to a semestered school in the south city. I'll start in January."

Jeff grinned. "Whew, I'm glad to hear that. I was worried you were going to drop out and not finish. Did Miller convince you?"

"No, well, sort of. I've been thinking lately that I should graduate and move on. And I don't mind helping Mom and Dad at home. Hey, I may get a job, part time, and make some money."

"Well, whatever you do, you know that I accept it," he said and took my hand from across the table. We stayed there talking till it got dark.

A week later I was signed up at another school and starting classes. Jeff came over the first night to see how it all went. He had news about Morgan.

"What happened?" I asked. We were sitting around a candle in my bedroom. My books were spread out on the bed where I'd been studying.

A slow smile spread across Jeff's face. "Well, Miller asked Morgan if he was the one spreading stories about you around the school. Morgan didn't answer yes or no. So Miller asked Kevin and he told him. Miller got really mad and stopped Morgan in the hall and told him he should be ashamed of himself. He then told the guidance office and they put on this senior assembly about gossip and rumors and how destructive they could be. Mr. Miller spoke at the assembly and said that gossiping and judging was far worse than any sexual impropriety. Morgan was totally isolated by this; everyone knew that he had blabbed about you. They all think he and Kevin and the rest of them are rats."

"I'm glad they got found out."

So that's how I ended up changing schools and changing friends in my last year of high school. Though my university entrance was delayed, I had a chance to get higher marks since I took fewer courses in the semestered terms. Jeff remained my boyfriend and I never went back to that school. A whole part of my life was wiped out.

Two terrible things happened to me: one was the sexual abuse after the club, and the other was my friends at school shunning me because of it. I can't remember the party because I was on a drug that night, though I am thoroughly ashamed, and wouldn't repeat what happened for anything. Yet it didn't damage me nearly as much as my best friends judging me, spreading stories, and cutting me out of their lives. I don't hate them – I don't think about them – but I know that I lost a part of myself that I'll never find again.

Commentary

Lauren is a gentle and intelligent girl who made some poor choices that almost derailed her life, a story that is reflected in high schools and colleges all over the country. Her self esteem isn't the highest, yet she is able to withstand a brutal rejection by her peers. These acts of bullying are usually swift and silent, and though many students might know about it, adults are the last to find out, if they ever do.

Lauren is also a victim of the guys in the date rape. Unfortunately, her "wasted" condition at the time means that she cannot remember what occurred with them and she never reports it out of shame and embarrassment about her own passivity.

Both kinds of bullying, the shunning and the date rape, are a common undoing of many students, who subsequently drop out of high school or university as a result.

Parents and teachers can help by being open minded and by listening without judgment to what their kids have to say. They can help kids to organize their lives so that they're not victims of peer pressure at parties and at school.

Peer pressure is a huge problem for most kids today and more attention needs to be paid to the forms it takes and to the effects of this social disease in senior public school and the early years of high school. Kids need positive role models, individuals who don't succumb to the sexual role modeling that dominates youth culture. Too often, the role model for girls is a starlet in skimpy attire, who's proud of her sexuality and going to show it. Often, a bright girl is confused about her identity, and boys, who are confused themselves, will take advantage of this.

The shunning seems old fashioned today, yet it goes on, on some level, in every school.

Activities and questions for discussion
(For adults and youths)

1. Remember a time when you felt pressured to do something you didn't want to do. How did you handle this and how did you feel about your response? Do you still feel pressured to do things you don't want to do? Discuss these answers with a partner or in a small group.

2. Write a story about a person who is a role model for you. Describe how they look, speak, act. Show why you want to be like them, and how successful you are in assimilating these qualities into your life.

3. Have you ever gossiped or shunned someone because of something you heard about them? What made you do this and what were the repercussions for you? How do you feel about this now?

8

Omar

"I can't take my report card home!"

I never thought that I would end up here at the technical high school enrolled in auto mechanics. It's like a dream come true! I spend the whole day tinkering with cars and I get marked for it. On my last report, I got all A's and B's. I love working with anything electric and especially engines and I seem to have a knack for knowing how to fix things. We just examined the engine of our teacher's antique; this 1954 Studebaker... what a beauty. They don't make cars like that anymore.

The tech students – some of them are animals. All day they fight and swear at the teachers. One pushed a teacher down the stairs and was expelled. They beat up other students; the police come by regularly. There are a lot more suspensions here, but I stay out of these guys' way and they don't bother me. Me and my friend keep our noses clean 'cause we want to do well now.

A year ago I was going nowhere fast at this academic high school, where I was an ESL student with all these other kids headed for university. I hated the place, these guys thinking they're hotshots with the girls and everything, the teachers coming down on you for not doing your homework and not having your soliloquy or whatever memorized. I was repeating the year, too, and still failing. Why? Because I hated the g d d   place with all my heart.

I hung out with this Russian guy, Sasha, and we had a blast and a half. He hated the school, too. We used to skip class and go out to smoke, come back and badmouth teachers who gave us grief for not doing our homework. Every class it was the same; we couldn't care less about anything we were studying.

Every morning we'd cruise the halls and visit with kids in different groups, or pick on guys like this Asian fag who had a stutter. In the cold weather, he wore this long scarf and funny hat, fancy ski jacket and shiny boots. We'd steal his scarf or hat and make him chase us to get it back. One day I grabbed it off him and ran, and he chased me, calling, "Hey yyyou gggguys, ggggive it back!!"

I yelled back, "Hey yyyyou ggguys, ggggive it back!! Hahahaha!" and tossed it to Sasha, who threw it on top of a locker so the guy had to ask a janitor to get it down for him. He was a rich kid; I'd seen his dad's flashy car when he dropped him off before school every day. I used to ask him to give me money for lunch. The guy gave me $10! He was such an artistic type. His only friends were girls in art class and these other queers, Trevor and Alan, who played in the school orchestra with him. One day we grabbed his precious trumpet and ran outside.

He went crazy: "Hey you guys, that's sssschool pppppproperty." We threw it on top of a snow bank. It was in its leather case so there was no damage, but he was almost crying. "Boo hoo!" I laughed, but Sasha said we'd better stop or he might tell the office on us. These Asian boys were easy to pick on, because they didn't want anyone to know they were wusses.

In English, we had to learn Romeo's speech from *Romeo and Juliet*. Okay, I liked this story, but I didn't like having to perform it in class. The teacher was this ditzy blonde, Ms. Green, who told us we had one week to learn it. I was repeating the year, so I knew all the books. But the year before I didn't learn the monologue, so why was I going to learn it this year? I mean, every time I started to say the lines, "With love's light wings did I o'erperch these walls…" they sounded so gay to me I couldn't get them halfway out of my mouth before I'd start to choke up with laughter. I wasn't going to stand up and be made a fool of in front of everyone.

All the other kids were rehearsing, murmuring their words to each other. One guy from Egypt, Naz, he thought he was so hot, he closed his eyes and put his hand on his heart and said his lines to these cute chicks near him, who giggled and laughed. Watching him made me sick. How could that idiot debase himself like that, speaking those words in that voice? Of course, Naz was very smart, though lazy as hell, and the teacher's favorite. He would get the best marks, hands down, for his speech.

And these girls speaking Juliet's lines, "O, Romeo, Romeo! Wherefore art thou, Romeo?..." Wow, they were hot. They'd whisper their lines as they practiced their monologues with their friends. Their skirts were so short and their legs so slender, their hair so long and shiny up in a pony tail, and they smelled like coconut or green apple shampoo. Ooooooo. How could I debase myself to them by saying Romeo's lines? I would try to learn them because I wanted the marks, but I couldn't concentrate. My brain would start drifting away, back to my country, where my friends and I used to play in the trees all day, like birds. We'd call from one tree to another, hooting out to each other, laughing so hard we'd fall upside down to the ground. I'd think about the forest near my grandmother's house, the smell of the trees and the sound of the birds, the ocean and the waves rolling in to the beach. Then Ms. Green would look over and I'd start whispering words, as if I were reciting the speech, because she also was marking us for the process of memorizing it.

Usually Sasha came halfway through a class, looked in the window beside the door, and signaled for me to come out for a smoke. I'd raise my hand and ask to be excused and Ms. Green always said, "Come right back." Me and Sasha would take off outside to smoke with the Russian kids. We'd smoke on the sidewalk just off the school property. Oh boy, those Russians used to skip class all day long and smoke their brains out, but they had better skills than I had and they still passed every term with good marks.

There was one hotshot named Igor; oh, he thought he was so cool, always in the latest jackets and shoes. Sometimes I'd insult him, call him "Mr. Cellophane," and he'd call me "Rathead," because I'm small, and we'd get a real thing going. I wanted to make him mad; I wanted him to blow his top. Yeah, I'd goad him, make fun of his girlfriends, call them "tramps" or "skanks," and he'd threaten, "I'll knock your teeth down your throat," and I'd grin, "Just try it." I'm a fast runner and he could never catch me. Sasha and others used to love it when I set Igor going, because they didn't like him so much.

But sometimes my younger brother Ibrahim, whose class was on that side of the building in the afternoons, would look out his classroom window and see me there smoking and skipping. Just in case he might tell my parents, I'd go into the school when the bell rang and grab him coming out of his class. I'd whisper, "Keep your trap shut or I'll get you again," and he'd look nervous because he remembered what I did the last time he squealed on me.

That happened at the end of the first term. We were getting our report cards so I skipped all my classes that day and me and Sasha went to the pool hall. Neither of us wanted to pick up our reports. By the time I got home, my brothers had showed theirs and my parents were waiting for mine. I tried to slip by them, but my father called out, "Hey, Omar, where is your report?" I came back and said, "Uh, I left it at school. I'll bring it after the holidays." Then Ibrahim said, "He skipped all day; he didn't even get his."

My father stood up and came over and grabbed me. "Hey, what did I tell you about studies, huh? Huh!?" He was pinching into my neck and twisting it at the same time.

"Oww, let go," I said, and he smashed me across the head with his fist. I doubled over to protect my head.

He was screaming, "What the f   am I going to do with you? You stupid good for nothing!" He kicked me and I fell over to one side. "You know what I said in September, that I wanted to see some good marks. You fail last year, you bring home s t marks and think that is okay. I warned you and you don't listen." He hit me again on my head. "I get up at five every f-----g morning to work in a factory for $15 an hour and your mother sews 14 hours a day just so you and your brothers can get a big education. Do you know how tired we are at night? But we tell ourselves that we are doing this for our sons so they can go to university. And last year you, the oldest, screwed up every day telling me you had no homework, no assignments, no tests, and then you never showed your report card," he plowed me again with his fist, "and we have to phone the school to get your marks which are all s t. This year I warned you that you have to study and you say that's what you're doing, but when I asked to see your notebooks, you left them in your locker. You weren't doing anything! How can you be a lawyer if you never study, huh? How can you be an architect? How can you so disrespect your parents?" He smashed me again twice and my mother said, "That's enough."

I cried and then I screamed at him, "I don't want to be a f   g architect. I want to be a mechanic. I told you."

"And work with your hands? Be a laborer? Do you think that I brought you all here for you to be laborers?" He looked around at my brothers, who had started crying when they saw me beaten. "You think I left my home, my people, my land to come here and have you screw around and waste yourselves? Well, answer me!"

Ibrahim said, "We are working hard, we like going to school."

My youngest brother, Abas, whispered, "I want to go to university."

My father said, "Get to bed, now. I don't want to see your face. If you failed again, I don't want you around here." But my mother began to cry, and begged him not to kick me out.

She came to my room and put some salve on my cuts. "Please, for my sake, study, and do what your father says. Stop fooling around."

"But I hate that school, I hate that academic stuff. I want to fix engines and I can make good money at it. A guy told me I could make $45 an hour."

My mother looked back over her shoulder and whispered, "But your father wants you to go to university, my son. That's why he brought us here and works at a job far beneath him. Can you imagine how he feels, packing boxes all day? You must work hard for him, if not for yourself."

"But I hate him, the way he yells at you and all of us. He's a monster." This made my mother cry, so I shut my mouth and said I would try.

When my brother came to bed, I pretended to be asleep, but then, when he was in bed, I got up and went over and sat on him and put my hand over his mouth. I grabbed his arm and bent it behind his head and pounded him with my other hand: "Keep your mouth shut or I'll make you regret that you ever opened it," I whispered. "Do you understand?" He nodded, shaking all over. After I left him and returned to my bed, I heard him crying into his pillow. So I knew that he wouldn't open his mouth again.

Of course, I failed my term, but I never showed my report to my dad because I knew he would explode. My mother signed it for me, but I had to go to the guidance office and my counselor, who was this old teacher, Ms. Jennings, asked me all these questions about my study habits and I told her a bunch of lies because I knew that's what she wanted to hear. She made me a study plan to follow, which had me doing two hours of homework a night and extra reading. I did it for one day and almost croaked it was so boring. I fell asleep over my notebook and ended up playing solitaire on the computer. My parents thought I was doing homework so that kept my father from slapping me around for a while.

But at school that winter term, the only thing I liked doing was my biography project, which was worth a lot of marks. I was doing mine on my hero, the world's greatest soccer player, Pele. This guy came from nothing, but his dad had been a good soccer player before he was sidelined by a leg injury, and he coached his son because he saw that he could be a champion. From the beginning, when he was only 11 years old, people knew that Pele was going to be a star. At 16, his very first game, he scored big and proved them right. He went on to play in four World Cups and score 1280 goals in 1360 games! He set the world record for hat tricks (92). He called soccer a "beautiful game" and came out of retirement in 1975 to make it popular in the U.S. I mean, he made it world famous. Like me, Pele was not huge. Just an average size, but he was blessed with speed.

Me and Sasha talked about soccer a lot. That's why I failed, I think. I had spent all of my energy on soccer so that I was exhausted when I came to classes. By February, Sasha and me were skipping big time. Either I'd go to his class and tap at the window beside his door or he'd do it to me. We were just horsing around, either smoking outside or teasing these girls because they were such flirts, although they were not allowed to have boyfriends. They always ate together on the steps at the back of the basement, so it was a good place to fool because teachers hardly ever came back there. We often went there after we'd eaten in the caf. We'd call out their names and tell them they were good looking, or ask if they'd give us some of their fries or pizza, or if they wanted to go out with us. One girl, Jasmin, used to bat her eyes and then tell us to go away, then giggle. She drove me crazy.

"Hey, you really want to do it," I said one day, just fooling. She started to scream, "What an animal!" but she was laughing, too. And then her friend told us to leave them and we said no, and they started whispering, and I didn't know what they were saying about us. Sasha said I should just ask her out, but I knew she'd say no. But there was a school dance coming up, a tea dance, which means after school, and I asked these chicks if they were going as it was chaperoned and all. They were all giggling and whispering and pretending they didn't care about it or us. Me and Sasha had it all planned that we'd score one girl each at the dance. I was so excited that I could barely sit in class and watch *A Streetcar Named Desire*, except that scene where Stanley attacked Blanche was a really hot one.

At the dance after school, me and Sasha were hanging out with the Russians and other kids in the cafeteria, which was all decorated with blue lights and silver mirrors that were hanging from the ceiling, reflecting everything around the room. It was quite sexy combined with the Janet Jackson hits the DJ was spinning. Sasha spied these girls we liked, talking and dancing together. We walked over and watched them as they lined up and waved their hands and shook their a   s.

I decided to ask Jasmin and walked over to her. "Want to dance?" She shrugged and pretended that she didn't know what I was saying, so I grabbed her hand and led her out to the floor and we started dancing. Sasha asked her friend Shaffie to dance.

We danced for the next half hour, until Jasmin said she wanted to go the washroom with Shaffie. So they walked off and we waited, but they didn't return. I decided to check for them at the washroom and stood by the door waiting for them. One girl told me to take off because she wanted to get in. I let her go by and then her boyfriend came over and asked me what I was doing. Sasha said we were waiting for some girls and then added, "What's your problem?" This guy looked like he was going to hit Sasha.

It all happened so fast. This big girl Angie came out and told me to "f off from the girls' washroom" and pushed me aside. I almost fell over, she was so big. I pushed her back and she screamed and fell down. She was badmouthing me and screaming, and I kicked her, not that hard, and Sasha was dragging me away when these other guys appeared, and some others after them, and asked what happened, and someone had a knife, which somehow ended up in my back, and then there were police cars and sirens. All because I was waiting for girls to come out of the washroom. And they weren't even in there after all; they'd left and gone home. Meanwhile, I was taken to Emergency and released because the cut wasn't very deep, about ten stitches. My parents were called and my dad came down to drive me home and he was crying because he heard that I was stabbed. "What happened? What the h you doing? Why did you hit a girl?" was all he could say. I pretended it hurt so much that I couldn't speak about anything.

The next day me and Sasha got suspended for fighting and I got to stay home legitimately, but a children's aid social worker came to visit our home. She said, "Your high school principal called and said they are concerned about Omar's safety at home. We have to investigate all the children who live here."

We all had to sit down and she asked a lot of questions. My mother and dad looked worried. I knew they were afraid we'd tell the social worker about my dad hitting me or my brothers. She asked if she could see my back, like she didn't believe me when I said, "No, nobody hit me at home," but there were these bruises left from when my dad beat me up the last time, before Christmas, when I had the bad marks.

"How did you get these?" she asked. I didn't answer. "Did someone beat you?" I didn't want to speak, so I shrugged like it didn't matter.

"Did your father do this?"

My mother was standing there and she nodded as if to say, "Tell the truth to the lady."

So I told her about my dad beating me for having not bringing home my report and for failing. My mother looked afraid, biting her lip and looking down. The social worker wrote notes down and said, "This kind of family violence is very hard on kids." My brothers said that my dad never did this, except once, and the social worker said, "Omar is old for high school, almost 19 years." She asked me, "What do you want to do after you finish?"

"I really want to study auto mechanics," I told her. "Why aren't you attending technical high school now?" she asked. I said, "My parents want me to be a lawyer. That's why they left their own country, for us to get a better life."

The social worker spoke to my father and told him, "You are not to hit your children; it's against the law. They will be watched for signs of abuse at school. If you do it again, they could be taken from you. Omar should not be at an academic school, but transferred to a school where he can study what he wants."

I hated to look at my dad's face when the social worker left. He looked so bent over and old and he cried and punched the walls. I cried. We all did. Then my dad said that I should try to finish my year at this high school, and that next year I might go to tech school if I still wanted. Later he went to the mosque and made a fast; he felt so bad that he wanted to cleanse himself. I did, too.

When I returned to school, I talked with Sasha about switching to tech and he wanted to as well. I visited my guidance counselor to pick up the information. "You're doing a smart thing, Omar," she said. We enrolled at the end of June. Before that happened, though, I handed in my 15 page project on Pele and got a pass on that, but failed the tests on the other books. Oh well, with the warm weather of May, it was hard to study, and we often skipped out and fooled with the girls at their lockers in the basement and outside under the trees where they ate their lunch. But we were careful not to be rude or to try any "hanky panky" as we had been warned by the office that next time we'd be expelled.

In the summer I got a job at Canadian Tire, where I pumped gas. During slow times, the boss, a guy called Bob, let me assist on some oil changes. He told me that I could keep the job in the fall. "Maybe you might work here when you graduate." He said he'd give me great references.

After I transferred to the tech school, I even went back to that high school to say hello and to visit. I kind of missed those academic kids after all. I also dropped by the guidance office to tell how I was doing at the tech school. I wanted to show that I wasn't a total loser.

My dad was even proud, too, after he saw my first term report. Believe it or not, he asked me to come with him when he bought his first car. It was a secondhand vehicle. He wanted me to okay it for him and asked me to check the engine. He only bought it after I pointed out a couple of defects that the dealership agreed to fix. It looks like things might be okay for me in this country after all.

Commentary

Omar is a typical bully who poses as a tough guy at school in order to camouflage what's really happening inside himself and at home. As long as he has a buddy like Sasha, who feels the same way, he projects his anger and despair on his teachers and fellow students.

Omar is being bullied at home and doesn't tell anyone, for fear perhaps of repercussions from his father. He also loves his mother and doesn't want to hurt her. He's stuck in the wrong program, because his parents are forcing him to live out their own dream, and he is afraid to do anything about it. In frustration, he lashes out at everyone around him. In one way, he's lucky that he can't even fake success at the academic school, so the chances of him freeing himself are better than for someone who can just go along and achieve a prescribed program. Only when a violent incident occurs at school does anyone discover what is going on at his home. Had a teacher or counselor sat him down and asked him carefully about his study habits and his home life, they might have been able to get him to open up. Unfortunately, it is very hard for the school to uncover this kind of abuse without a trigger incident, or bodily scars, or marks that invite personal questions.

Some teachers might write this kind of student off as a goof who has little ability, and be frustrated by his presence in their classroom as he seems incorrigible. Since his parents don't support his dream of attending tech school, it is almost impossible for teachers or counselors to do anything with or for him. He's his own worst enemy and he has his supporter to allow him to get away with it.

Most bullies find a group of supporters who in some way egg them on and who support, either silently or actively, their picking on the undefended student. Sometimes negative behavior can be averted if a teacher can appeal to these supporters and inspire them to stop the bully, walk away, or report what he or she is doing. Since Sasha is Omar's buddy and supporter, talking to him and showing him how he is hurting other students, as well as Omar, might cause him to stop supporting Omar when he is bullying others. Often, though, supporters are afraid to stand up to the bully. Usually, the supporter is also hiding his or her own aggression.

The big problem for most adults is figuring out which one is the bully, as both bullies and supporters are very good at concealing their actions and transferring blame to others. Teachers, therefore, have to ask about what's going on, closely observe kids in the halls and on the playgrounds, and mix students up in the classroom so as to break up cliques and friendships that protect and engender bullies.

Parents have a harder time because children like Omar will lie about schoolwork and tend not to trust anyone. The best approach is to listen without judgment when the child *does* want to talk and to involve the child in family chores and activities.

While some immigrant parents may have been allowed to abuse a child in their home culture, their *kids* quickly find out that this is not condoned, by law, in Canada. Usually, however, they are loathe to report their parents and get them into trouble. Most students feel deeply ashamed if they are being bullied by a parent and do not want to tell anyone about it. These kids need a lot of support and understanding from teachers and other supervisors.

When a family undergoes a lot of stress due to divorce or death, shifting economics, or changing countries and cultures, children often suffer the fallout and great effort must be taken to listen to and support their desires. Success is more likely if the child is doing what they enjoy and are good at.

Questions for discussion

(These questions are intended for discussion at school, or at home, or with study groups.)

1. What can someone do if they are being bullied by their parent(s)? Who can they talk to? How can they help themselves and their family? What message do they need to give to their parents?
2. How can students show their parents what they need in order to be successful in their studies and social life?
3. Why do kids support bullies, either by silence or by action?
4. Name four ways to defend the victim of a bully, in ways that will support them without a lot of embarrassment.
5. Name four ways to stand up to friends who are bullies.

9
Natalya

"All I wanted was to grow up and get out of there."

I don't think that my parents had any idea how hard our home life was on us kids before everything fell apart for me in Grade 8. They thought that since they treated me and my older brother well – they called Dimitri "dearest boy," and me, "the sweetest angel," and said "everything we do is for you kids" – we would be happy and ignore everything that went on between them. What they didn't know was that by the time I was ten, I would wake up every morning and think, "If I can just get through today," and every night, "only eight more years and I'll be free."

It wasn't all bad. I do have to thank them for my academic success, because school was like heaven compared to home, which felt like… well, honestly… a prison of hate.

It was so crazy. Though they adored us, they seemed to despise each other. Why did they ever get married? My mum told me, "We were born in the same town in Romania, started going together at 14 and got married at 17. We didn't know any better."

Dad added, "We would have divorced but… then you and your brother came along."

Sometimes I'd look at their photo albums from Europe; I'd look at the pictures of them when they were young and beautiful, fresh and happy, and devoted to each other. Their wedding picture: my mother in a white lace gown, my father and his friends in their black suits, surrounded by all these old relatives on the church steps. They certainly looked in love, perched on their bicycles, waving goodbye as they went off on their honeymoon tour. What happened, I wondered, as I gazed at those images.

Now they were tired, grumpy people, who worked hard to pay cash for everything. Mom cooked low budget but delicious meals, and somehow we always had good looking clothes. She kept the house super clean. You could eat off her floor. Neither of them ever struck us, but, ever since I was tiny they bickered and cursed at one another: "I never said that!" "Don't talk to me in that tone!" "Did you take your ugly medicine again?" "All you do is complain!" "Nobody really likes *you!*" A day rarely passed without them trading insults: "I never said that!" "You did so, you witch!.." "You stupid oaf!" "Can't you ever do anything right?"

If my father didn't like the way my mum looked at him as she spooned out his noodles, he would get up and scrape his food into the garbage. When he cooked something good, she found fault with it and he'd say, "Then get out of here!" and she'd run to their room or go outside.

One day, she took scissors and cut up all his shirts so that he didn't have anything to wear to work and had to go out to Salvation Army for replacements.

"If I wasn't stuck with you, I might have a chance to be happy," he said.

"I wished you'd go and give us some peace," she shouted back.

When they fought like this, Dimitri and I would roll our eyes, plug our ears, and sometimes plead, "Just stop, will you!" and sometimes they would, for a little while.

Often, they turned to us to take their side against the other: "Look, do you see how she lies?" Or she might say, "He's ruined my life, you can see." We were the battlefield on which they fought.

Strange as it seems, we were their best friends. They always hugged and kissed us when we got up or came home after school. We helped Mom with her baking and housework because she worked as a cleaning lady, and after school we did our homework in the kitchen while she made dinner. Dad asked us to go with him everywhere he went, even camping, hiking, and fishing in a provincial park. Most winter weekends, if he could, he skated and tobogganed with us too.

Mom and Dad each believed that that they were the superior parent and our favorite. After a school concert or parents' night, they'd even fight about our talents being related to their own side of the family.

Countless nights, I fell asleep with the sound of angry shouts breaking the dark silence, and many mornings began the same way. On the weeks when they didn't speak, we had to live with the chill of their silence, and the weeks when they got along and laughed at each other's jokes, we crept about, nervous for when the war would resume.

Since our home life was unpredictable, Dimitri and I lived from one day to the next, hiding in our own play, or, as we got older, in our talks, reading, and schoolwork. We told each other our secrets. We were best friends.

When I was ten, school was my total refuge, my ticket to freedom. I loved walking to that happy red brick building with my brother, and standing in the schoolyard waiting for the bell to ring. That bell lifted my heart. Now I could go in and sit down and be totally free of my parents' problems for eight hours. I loved my teacher and listened intently to her instructions, happily opening my reader or notebook and absorbing the lesson, whatever it might be. Silent reading hour was my favorite time, when I could put my nose in a book and escape to some imaginary place, people, or animals.

My Grade 5 teacher, Mrs. Arthur, became my role model. A tall Canadian woman with lovely dimples in her cheeks, she was calm and fair, always spoke in a low and pleasant tone, and disciplined students in a way that made kids obey without resentment. I worked hard to win her approval, to be the best in writing, math, art, and science. A few kids called me a teacher's pet, but I was rarely picked on because my brother was always nearby and would have defended me had anyone ever tried.

I also never wanted to be popular or to be anyone's "best friend" like so many other kids. To me, being a best friend meant being involved with people's problems and I had enough of that at home. I also didn't want any kid finding out what my parents were really like. I don't think any of the teachers guessed my misery; they thought that I was a happy and industrious student.

I would never have told on my parents, no matter what. On weekends, when they sometimes drank wine or beer, their fights got worse and things like glasses, plates, and chairs got broken. Dimitri and I hid in our rooms with our music turned up loud.

But outside the house my parents always acted polite. Our neighbors and friends would never have guessed how they really were with each other. Even when our relatives came to visit from Europe, they both put on a great front of family solidarity. Only my brother and I knew that after the visit, one of them would start, "Why did you tell the so and so that you were doing well? It sounded so phony." Or, "You always smile in that stupid way of yours. Everybody thinks you're phony. You look ridiculous." Dimitri and I looked out the windows and cringed at the sound of their twisted words.

We went along with this charade until Grade 8, when I, like lots of kids, began to change, and to get terrible headaches as well. The doctor said they were caused by tension and asked if anything was bothering me. Not thinking, I said, "No." But gradually, I, who could study for hours the previous year, found it hard to concentrate on my homework. The headaches lasted for hours, making me moody and ill tempered – one day happy, the next day miserable. I started calling my parents by their first names, Anna and Stefan. When they asked why I was doing that, I just answered, "You're just people like anyone else, why can't I call you by your real names." They didn't stop me, worried as they were about my headaches. They were concerned that it might be a brain tumor or something. Dimitri still called them Mom and Dad.

Sometimes I was plain rude to them. "Just get off my back!" I said, if they asked too many questions about my health. I changed my style and dyed my hair black, and then green. I wore tighter jeans and shorter sweaters, and makeup. Every day as I stood at the mirror getting dressed, I carefully outlined my eyes and darkened my lashes and put on pale lipstick. If my parents said that it was too much, I would shrug, "Whatever," and walk out of the house.

At school, in the gifted program, I was one of the three best students. My math and science teacher, Mr. Bertram, who had also taught me in Grade 7, asked, "Why are you so withdrawn, Natalya?"

I just looked at him and blinked, I couldn't think of what to say. The only person I trusted was Dimitri; I spent a lot of time in his room talking about school, music, kids.

Our parents were still fighting and the sound of their voices was horrible, especially when I had a headache. I started to hang out with some kids in my class who also had parent problems. Megan's parents were divorced and she had to switch her stuff back and forth between their homes on the weekends. Often her dad was with his girlfriend, and Megan had to babysit her kids, who were brats and took her stuff. Another student in our group, Shawn, had heavy drinking parents, who were often so drunk they never noticed that he stole liquor out of their cabinet and shared it with friends.

I liked these kids. They didn't tell lies and put on a cool act like most other kids did, as if everything was perfect. Shawn and Megan hung out with me and Dimitri in the schoolyard and sometimes in the park. Megan was dark and pretty, but also insecure. She was always full of family troubles. Her aunt got picked up for shoplifting, and her mom got drunk and lost her license, then she lost her job. "I hate my mom," she'd say, and "I can't trust my dad." Sometimes she didn't want to go home, so I stayed out with her till after dark and then walked her home.

Shawn and I liked each other. He was cute, funny, and weird, and he was a wicked cartoonist. He used to draw comics about our teachers and the other kids. I never got bored watching him draw, which he did most of the time. I felt bad for him when he got depressed, smoked up and drank with older kids, who were friends of his sister's. I also didn't want to get into trouble. Kids at my school kind of shunned him, because he had tattoos of clenched fists and crossed knives on his arms, grew his hair long, and always wore black. Sometimes he was sarcastic to teachers too, and argued with them about legalizing drugs, and sometimes he had to go down to the office for skipping. Once he got suspended. Mr. Bertram even warned me one day, "You could get in trouble hanging out with Shawn. Be careful. You can't save everyone, you know." I wondered if Mr. Bertram knew about Shawn's family. Shawn was a smart kid whose family was messed up and he didn't really have a home. He made my problems seem minor. Dimitri and I hung out with him and listened to these garage bands that he liked.

One night, while I was studying for a math test in my room, I heard my parents fighting about something. My head was aching as well and I didn't feel strong, but I had to study because this test was worth 50 percent of our term. I put on my Walkman to drown them out, but then I couldn't concentrate and my head got worse. I hoped it wasn't going to be another migraine, because I wouldn't be able to write my test. Then the phone rang and it was for me. "Hi," I said.

The speaker didn't answer. "Hi again," I repeated.

Shawn's voice sounded far away. "I might be going away, I can't take this anymore."

"Shawn, what's the matter?"

"I just don't think that I can go on any longer."

My heart started pounding. "Don't be negative. You'll be all right."

"I've taken a lot of pills and booze." He was slurring his words.

"Shawn, do you need help?"

"No, I don't think so now."

"Shawn, don't say that. I'm going to call the hospital. Just stay where you are."

I hung up the phone. My head pounded and I felt nauseous. My parents were screaming and I thought that I was going to faint, but all I could think about was helping Shawn. I called 911 and told them Shawn had taken an overdose and needed an ambulance to his house. I then told Dimitri and he looked shocked: "Wow, he must be hurting bad. It's good that you phoned 911."

My mother called my name. "Natalya! Come down here now."

"O god, I wonder what these idiots want," I said to Dimitri.

When I came downstairs, my mom was crying. "Your father says I'm insane and weak and driving you all crazy." My father's face was red and shiny. He'd been drinking again.

"Look, Mom, I can't take this. I'm studying for a test and my friend might die so I can't help you."

My father ignored what I said. "Hey, she is crazy, says that I spend all the money on myself. Who is she kidding? I pay the mortgage on this house, and the car, and she says I am spending money on some girlfriend. This is a lie and she is crazy."

My mother snarled, "Look who is lying. His pockets are full of receipts for bars and motels."

He waved his hand and swore at her. Dimitri appeared on the steps listening to their tirade. My head was hurting so much that I had to press my whole palm against it hard to keep it from throbbing.

I spoke in a loud, clear voice to drown them out. "Mom and Dad, stop this and listen to what I am saying." They turned around to face me. "My friend Shawn has just overdosed and is probably in Emergency by now, but all you can do is think about yourselves. I want you to know that I can't stand this anymore. All of my life, you have fought and argued with each other and made us take sides and we are sick of it. It's killing me and Dimitri. Sometimes I can't even think anymore because of your fighting. I hate being in this house; I want to leave as soon as possible. You two should not be together; you are destroying each other. Look at me, with my migraines! Do you know how bad they feel? Yet you keep on. Every night in this house is like walking in a minefield. Stop thinking about yourselves and start thinking about what you are doing."

My parents stared at me. My father said, "I know it's bad for you and Dimitri. Don't you think I feel guilty about it? I came here to make a new life for us all. But your mother keeps it up, criticizing me and..."

"Then why do you stay together?"

My mother said, "I'd break up happily, my child, if I could afford it. But I can't. I don't earn enough to keep you and Dimitri, or I'd have left him long ago."

"That's right. She's just here for the money," my father snapped, "that's the truth."

"Stop right now! I can't live with this. You are destroying us with your bickering. I never want to have a family, I never want to get married, I can't stand what I see. If it weren't for Dimitri, I couldn't live here. I don't know what to do. But I do have a math test tomorrow and it's worth 50 percent of my term mark. So would you both just shut up??"

I went back upstairs and phoned Shawn's house. His little brother, Liam, answered and when he knew that it was me, he said, "Shawn's gone to the hospital in an ambulance with Kyla (their older sister)."

"Good," I said. "Do you know how he is?"

"Yea, Kyla just phoned and said he's going to be okay."

"You'd better go to bed, Liam," I said.

When I went up to my bedroom, my head hurt so much I couldn't study and I had to lie down. So much for my math term.

Dimitri and I walked to school the next day. "Let's move out," I said.

"Where would we go?"

Since our relatives all lived in Europe, it was hard. We really had no place to run to.

"Good luck on your test," he said, as we went into the school.

The test was really hard and covered work that we were to prepare for the night before. My head started to swim. I looked over and saw that Shawn's seat was empty. The other students were working away bent over their papers, pens scratching. When I looked back at my paper the numbers swam all over the page. I tried to focus by closing my eyes and thinking of the page in the book that I'd been reading the night before. Nothing came into my mind. I put my head down on my desk and covered it with my arms. I wished the floor would open up and my desk could descend to another world below.

"Are you all right, Natalya?" Mr. Bertram was crouching down by my desk.

"Huh? Oh, I… uh… must… uh… have fallen asleep." I sat up and looked at my blank paper. Tears came into my eyes and I started crying.

"You can go to the washroom if you want," Mr. Bertram said.

I got up and left and went to the washroom and washed my face and waited till the end of the period, when the test was over, before I returned. The other kids all filed out of the room, their faces pale, most of them murmuring that it had been really difficult. I went up to Mr. Bertram's desk.

"What happened? I notice you didn't write anything? Was it too hard?" He looked worried, as I was the best math student in the class.

"Uh, it was hard, but I had a terrible night and I couldn't think. I went blank. That's never happened to me before."

"Are you under any stress?"

I told him about Shawn and he nodded. "Yes, that would do it, but you know, Shawn's problems aren't your concern, at least you shouldn't be this worried that you forget about your own studies, especially when you are a gifted student."

I said, "It isn't just Shawn. It's my parents. They're driving me crazy and I don't know how I can go on with them."

It was the first time I had ever told anyone about them. My lips trembled and my hands shook. But Mr. Bertram said, "How are they driving you crazy?"

I started to cry again and couldn't stop. "Sit down," he said. It was lunchtime and everyone was in the cafeteria. The halls were silent.

"My parents fight and argue all the time, they never stop, and they make it impossible for me to think."

"How long has this been going on?"

In a small voice I answered, "Since I was little. Me and my brother can't stand it. It's killing us. But we don't have enough money to leave."

Mr. Bertram said, "Would you like to talk with the school social worker? It will be very private, but that's what they're there for. Perhaps that would help you and your family."

I looked up at him. "I think that Shawn and his family need help, so do others. They just don't tell anyone about it."

"Well, they're probably being loyal, like you have been. But it's misplaced loyalty. You shouldn't have to put up with this kind of abuse. Yes, that's what it is. It's very good that you are telling me this. Your parents need help."

The next week I had my first appointment with the school social worker, Ms. Chevalier. She congratulated me for telling my teacher. "That took nerve and courage. You have been protecting your parents like so many kids do, and have been suffering for that. Let's talk about these headaches that keep you from studying."

It was after that talk that she got me into a headache clinic at the hospital and I found out that my body was all tense and that I didn't even breathe. I learned to breathe for the first time in my life, which was weird to me. I don't mean that I never breathed before, but, due to the screaming and tension between my parents, I held my breath a lot and only released it through my nose, so my breath wasn't getting enough oxygen to my brain, and that's why I had migraines. I found out that I'd also been "holding" myself together for years.

My brother also came to see the social worker and we started telling her about my parents. She said, "You've been victims of their bad marriage and it has clouded your life. You've been afraid to be happy and enjoy having friends and being relaxed, the way you should at your age."

My parents were so broken up about my health that it caused them to seek treatment for themselves. Ms. Chevalier got them into a family therapy program, which, thankfully, was free. She also interviewed Shawn and assigned him to see another great social worker, Mr. Beeton, who came every week to visit him at our school. Megan started seeing him, too.

Our French teacher, Ms. Chartrand, asked us to start a social chat group that met after school to talk about our lives and our relationships. Ms. Chartrand became our advisor. Dimitri and other younger students joined, too. We watched videos and discussed problems at home and at school. It was amazing the number of students who had problems like ours, and our group helped a lot of kids to be honest about their lives in a way they never would have been otherwise. We found out that while we might not be able to change our parents, we could change our reactions to them.

At the end of Grade 8, my parents got a separation, but one that gave them a lot of support. For example, my mom could work as a cleaning lady, but still get money for us. Even my father could see that it was the best scenario for me and Dimitri. We would live with my mom and be with my dad on the weekends.

If I hadn't told my teacher about my problems at home, then none of this would be happening. I sometimes still have bad nightmares and I have to stop and make myself breathe, but at least I know now how to breathe and I don't have to keep a lid on my life.

Commentary

Natalya is a bright, solid student, who copes with a fractious family life by achieving high marks and a good reputation with the teachers at school. This all works until the stress of keeping so much hidden breaks out in her migraine headaches. She is living two opposite lives and that burden also causes her to seek out negative relationships with needy people at school.

Eventually, she ends up helping herself by telling her teacher. Luckily, her teacher is sensitive and aware enough to ask about what is going on at home.

Natalya's story is all too common. Many kids cover up their parents' addictions and other destructive behaviors by either becoming over achievers, or conversely, by bullying other kids at school, or by acting out in anti social ways. Teachers need to be aware of the stress that all kids carry into school, regardless of the front they may present. Teachers need to be watchful and considerate of the signs of family dysfunction, and create opportunities for disclosure and release. A truly nurturing teacher will teach their subject *and* be aware of what is happening within the students.

One way to help students come out of themselves is to pair opposites together, so that an extrovert and an introvert might support one another and draw the other out. Give students chances to make presentations in class so that everyone gets an opportunity talk in front of the class and perhaps reveal some of their own fears and inhibitions.

Parents need to recognize that their moods and behaviors have a big influence on their kids. Whether parents realize it or not, kids absorb what is going on around them. They may not reveal how they are affected, but their parents' problems definitely impact them.

Parents need to watch their own methods of quarreling and, if things seem out of hand, get help and show kids that these problems can be dealt with and changed. Parents live with many heavy pressures, including mortgage payments, jobs, and family relationships, and it's not surprising that sometimes they may need to talk and seek a professional for advice. Had Natalya's parents done something years before, they might have saved their son and daughter a torment that will probably affect them for the rest of their lives.

Questions for discussion

(These can be used with small groups, or with a class of adults or senior public school/high school students.)

1. Describe three main stresses that you grew up with in your home. How were these handled by you and your parents? How did these affect your behavior at school and in the community?
2. Describe or show two ways that families could handle stress in a positive way for everyone.
3. Describe a problem you are keeping a "lid" on. How is this affecting you now? How could you release what's inside of you, in a creative way?

10
Alexander

"I just wanted to fit in."

I'm not sure why I got tied up with those guys, but I guess I wanted to fit in and they were a powerhouse in the school. I was a new student and ESL as well, except that I could speak and write English well enough to take some mainstream classes. At first, kids made fun of me because of my loud, clear voice and my European haircut. They thought I was pretty gay and teased me in gym class and stuff, calling me "Pretty Boy." I ignored them at first and worked hard to get good marks and get along with everyone. I wanted to do well, both in sports and in schoolwork, and I wanted to be accepted.

I was used to being the new kid and having to work hard to fit in. How many schools had I attended? Almost too many to count. I began school in China, living with my grandparents, while my parents studied abroad. Then I joined them and attended schools in Switzerland, Boston, the USA, and Norway. Recently, they got divorced and were teaching in universities in Europe, so I came to Canada to get my final year of high school and to attend university. I lived with my uncle, who didn't really know me. Though my parents phoned every week, I was lonely.

I tried out for the soccer team and made it first cut because I am quite good in sports. I was made goalie. It was at the practices that I got to know Adam, who was a good player as well. He led the team with his nimble footwork, his aggressive energy, and his metal voice, which cut through the game: "Get to the ball!" "Kick it! Kick it!" "Pass it! Pass it!" If guys missed a pass he made to them, he wasn't shy about letting them know what he thought of them after the game. He was tough and hard and played full throttle without letting up. Once he got the ball, it was hard to stop him.

All the players respected him and wanted his approval. I was secretly pleased when he included me in his group of friends. We gathered in the halls in the morning and shot the breeze, gossiping about world soccer and local players, and flirting with cute girls who passed by. Adam was supremely confident, with a flashing smile that exposed his straight white teeth. His best friend was a guy called Greg, who lived near him and also played on the team. It was to Greg that he directed most of his jokes or opinions and Greg always responded by laughing. If one of us wasn't listening, he'd jab us in the ribs: "Adam's talkin'. Listen up, dude!" The other guys, Jack and Manny, seemed equally in awe of Adam, though they wouldn't have admitted it. We were all cool, which meant that we didn't ever look needy or vulnerable. I concealed my marks from them, as I knew mine were at least 20 percent higher than theirs.

Every day the same scenario took place. Adam and his buddies gathered in the hall. Leaning against the wall of lockers, striking cool poses, they joked and eyed anyone who walked past, remarking upon them in some non verbal way: a lift of an eyebrow, a mimicking gesture, a funny face, in a mock insult way. They did this to most everyone, except for a Chinese boy named Edward, who, for some reason, they disliked.

Edward was not athletic or popular. He and his friend Simon were in my math class and sometimes I played chess with them in a corner at lunch. Since we often talked in Mandarin, I made certain that I did this when Adam, Greg, and friends weren't around. I couldn't understand why Adam picked on Edward, but he made ridiculous clucking sounds whenever Edward walked by, or called out his name in a falsetto voice. Edward looked straight ahead and kept on walking, as if he didn't hear. This made Adam even more determined and he would call out, "What a twit!"

I never said anything when Adam made fun of Edward in the hall. Why I should step in, I rationalized; it wasn't like he was my best friend. But I also felt uneasy and wondered vaguely if Adam was picking on Edward instead of picking on me.

One day, I walked into the washroom and caught Greg and Adam intimidating Edward. "Hey, ch k, what are you doing? You think you're smart, eh?"

One of them shoved Edward to the other wall and Greg laughed. "What are you going to do about it, huh Eddie? Are ya goin' to fight us?"

Edward removed his glasses and they fell into two pieces in his hands, broken by the slam against the wall.

"Oh dear, he's broke his glasses. Now he won't be able to see the blackboard."

Edward fumbled with his glasses and tried to fix them, but it was useless. Without them, he could hardly see. He walked unsteadily towards the door.

"Uh, if you mention this to anyone, we'll break something else," Adam said, and Greg gave an unpleasant giggle.

Edward walked out and they turned to me. "Hey, Alex, how ya doin? What's goin' down?"

I washed my hands and mumbled, "Nothing," and left with them. Nobody mentioned Edward, as if what I saw hadn't really happened. But my heart thudded and I was as frightened as if they had shoved *me*.

Every day when Edward passed by us, Adam snickered or made a gesture, which Edward continued to ignore as if Adam didn't exist. Greg laughed and said, "I don't think he cares, dude."

Adam's face tightened and he punched Greg lightly on the arm. "He's keepin' his nose clean."

Again I felt this strange fear and nervousness. I couldn't look them straight in the eyes and I couldn't put my words together.

The next time I played chess with Edward, he asked, "Why didn't you tell those guys to stop bugging me the other day?"

My face flushed and I didn't answer for a minute. Then I mumbled, "Uh, I didn't know what it was about; I didn't want to interfere."

Edward glared at me through his taped glasses. "Oh, yeah, you think I believe that? You're as afraid of him as anyone."

"Do you think so?" I replied, belligerently, though I suspected he was right.

I changed the topic to the game we were playing and was relieved when the bell rang and we could go to classes.

I couldn't shake off the look in Edward's eyes; it was so sad and hurt. I promised myself that if it happened again I would stand up to Adam and Greg and not let them get away with it. But the next week I saw Adam talking with Edward in the cafeteria. I wondered what they were talking about and came over. Greg joined me and we stood beside Adam, who was saying, "I was wonderin' if you could help me with my math homework. I didn't get my homework done and we have, uh, the same teacher, different periods. He'll never know if you give me your work."

I knew that lots of kids at school copied assignments from other kids, but Edward was the top math student. He'd come second in the provincial competition. He wasn't going to give it to Adam.

Edward shook his head. "No, I don't want to give it to you. Do your own."

Adam grimaced and gave a little laugh, "Look, dude, I told you. I don't have it done. Now are you goin' to give it to me or what?"

Edward gathered up his papers into his backpack. "I got to go."

Adam blocked him from getting up. "If you don't give me the answers, I'll make sure you won't be walking to school for a long time."

Edward shouted, "Hey, you're threatening me!"

Adam laughed. "Take it easy, dude, I was kidding you."

Greg added, "Calm down. We're joking."

Edward looked at me and said, "Are you going to hang around with thugs like these?"

I shrugged and said, "Whatever."

Edward walked away and Adam said, 'What an a h ! I asked him for one little thing and he freaks out. Go figure!"

Greg echoed him. "Ya, what a f g nerd."

I tried to speak, but nothing came out. I pushed my tongue forward to my teeth to make a sound, but nothing… My words shriveled in my mouth.

The guys took my silence as an assent of their attack on Edward. I could barely see when I walked out of the cafeteria; my eyes were burning with shame that this guy Adam had me so afraid I had lost my own will.

"Hey, buddy," Adam said as I went to my locker. "I was wondering if you'd be a buddy and lend me your math homework. I won't keep it for long." He flashed his huge smile. "Well?"

I dug the homework out of my backpack and gave it to him.

"Hey, thanks a bunch!" he said, and went to the library to copy it.

I felt like throwing up. I leaned my head against my locker. I had never felt so lost in my whole life. I was sorry I had ever come to this country to get a better education. What a joke!

An hour later, Adam found me and returned my homework, "Hey, thanks, man."

"S'okay."

I just wanted to get home and climb under the sheets and go to bed, but I had a big soccer game after school and I had to stay for it. We all got out of class an hour early. In the dressing room as we changed into our uniforms, Adam came over and spoke to me in a low voice. "Hey, thanks for the homework. I got 10 out of 10 and I needed those extra marks. I owe ya."

I didn't answer. I didn't like talking much before a game. It interfered with my concentration.

We played hard and well, and won the game. Adam and Greg whooped and shouted as we all went back to the dressing room after shaking hands with the other team. Later, I overheard him and Greg talking as they showered. "Yeah, first let's grab us some brewskies and maybe afterwards, find him and teach him a lesson he's asking to learn." I wondered who they were talking about, but pretended that I didn't hear.

As I left the change room, I waved goodbye to them and cut out for home. I fell asleep almost as soon as I hit my bed. I was so tired I didn't eat the supper my uncle left for me until the next day. Holed up in my room, I spent the weekend studying and doing assignments. On Sunday, my mother phoned and asked how I was doing. "Okay, I guess," I said.

"Just okay?" my mother asked.

"Well, there's a lot of work."

"Would you like to come over for a visit? Stockholm is beautiful. The air is so clear."

"Uh, no thanks."

I wanted to say "help me" to my parents, "I'm drowning here," but the words didn't make it up my throat and through my mouth.

"Bye, Mom, I love you," I said.

On Monday, I returned to school and met the guys hanging out in the hall. "Hey, Alex, man!" they cried. "How are you?"

This is what I had craved, to belong to a group of popular kids who were in, who created the action. And here I was, accepted as part of such a group and it was killing me. I was bored for one thing; they never had anything interesting to say. All their talk was about other people. I was also getting more in touch with what a coward I was and it sickened me.

"Did you hear about Adam?" Jack asked.

"No, I just got here, what?"

"Him and Greg got picked up by the police for harassment! They got drunk after the game on Friday and went to Edward's apartment to hassle him. The building Super caught them snooping around the back of the building and called the cops. They were caught with steel pipes in their hands. It's incredible!"

So that's what they were planning in the shower, to go and lure Edward out of his apartment and beat him up. The thought of it was revolting.

"What's the matter dude? You don't look too well."

"I'm okay," I muttered. "Lots of homework on the weekend, that's all."

I walked down the hall and found Simon and Edward huddled in their usual corner playing chess with another guy. "Hey!" I said.

They nodded and kept their eyes on the game. I was wondering if I should say something to Edward, but maybe he already knew about Adam. I watched his face as he contemplated the chess board, the fine straight nose, the keen dark eyes framed by the bandaged glasses, the black hair hanging over his forehead. What had I been thinking, craving popularity with guys who were so insecure that they couldn't accept a guy with a real mind and an independent spirit? I bent my head over the chess game and chanted to myself, "I am a free man. I don't need to be popular. I just need one real friend."

When Adam and Greg returned to school the next day, they were full of bravado and called out to me, "Hey, where ya goin'?"

"I've got a chess game waiting," I replied.

"A *chess* game?" Adam chortled.

"Yeah, it's one of my favorite games. I always played it back home." I pulled myself up to my full height and waved, "See you guys."

Edward said nothing when I sat down with them. He was concentrating on his next move in the chess game. I knew that, aside from soccer, I was through with hanging out with the popular kids. I felt lucky to get away as easily as I had. Who knows what trouble they might have got me into? I heard that both of them were charged and might now have criminal records. But more than that was the shudder I felt thinking about what they might have done to Edward and how guilty I would feel that I had done nothing.

When the game ended, I walked down the hall with Edward. "Hey, man, I want to apologize that I never helped you with those guys. I wanted to, I just couldn't. I was, uh, well, afraid, and I'm sorry."

Edward smiled. "It's hard to have convictions and stick by them," he said. "Somehow, I knew you'd come to your senses."

"Yeah, but I found out that I'm a real coward and I want to change. That's why I want to hang around with you."

Edward pointed to his head and tapped it. "You're a smart guy," he said as we turned into the math class.

Commentary

Alexander, an immigrant student, is on his own and struggling with loneliness, fear, and a desire to be accepted and popular. He is sophisticated, having been educated in Europe as well as in Asia. He is living between two cultures and is not sure which one he wants to belong to, as he does speak well and can "pass" in Canada. As a child of divorced parents and having lived in so many places, he is highly aware of his need to fit in, or not.

In Adam, Alexander meets both a talented athlete and a racist, insecure bully, who has to have the control of a group. Like a lot of bullies, Adam lacks compassion and sensitivity to the feelings of others, although he is acutely sensitive to each person's uniqueness. Perhaps he picks on Edward because he doesn't value Adam's popularity and strength; or maybe his bullying represents an indirect rejection of Alexander's roots. Adam's bullying and Alexander's fear of speaking up and stopping him, is disturbing and hidden behavior that commonly goes on at private and public schools, high schools, and among and between most cultures.

Alexander "supports" Adam at first, because he wants to be accepted by the power group. When he finally *does* realize that their power is destructive to others, he wants to speak out and do the right thing, but he can't. He doesn't have the practice or the strength to stand up to someone like Adam, even though the victim is an acquaintance and someone from his own race. Though he tries, Alexander can't seem to conjure the strength to speak out against what he knows is wrong. This fear of confronting the bully, of expressing disapproval of bullying actions, is a huge problem in schools today.

Greg, Manny, and Jack also support the bully and identify with him, though they might not be as aggressive if they acted on their own. In fact, it is the solidarity in numbers that gives most bullies their strength. The "herd mentality," which exists in much of school life, means that everyone conforms to an unwritten rule – you don't "tell" what's going on with bullying. This mentality is strengthened by a fear that the bully will find out if you tell, and will get revenge. It is also strengthened by a "mob rule" acceptance of bullying as a "cool" fact of life that *should* be secret.

Adam dominates school life by obvious as well as subtle kinds of bullying, all of it supposedly joking. Such a bully uses swearing, threats, and name calling against sensitive or imaginative kids, making their lives very unpleasant.

Teachers and parents can help kids enormously with this problem by encouraging them to think for themselves, to think out loud, to express their opinions, and to not be afraid to fail or to make a mistake by saying the wrong thing. Gain the trust of kids by talking and listening, and by making a real effort to understand what they're saying. Get them thinking about and discussing real issues that pertain to them. Try to deflate the pressure to be popular by getting kids interested in other age groups and cultures. Help them to be aware of how hard it is for new Canadians to live between two cultures. Take time to get to know the kids you interact with (both immigrants and long-term residents) and their feelings about this country.

If you see signs that a child is being bullied, take time to talk with him or her gently about this. If you feel it's important, call the parent(s) and discuss it with them.

Activities and questions for discussion
(For youth and adult groups)

1. Tell about a time when you wanted to belong to a powerful group or organization, and what you learned by being a member. Was it a positive or negative experience? Were you able to speak your mind easily when you had something to say?
2. Have you ever been discriminated against because of your race or color? What did you learn in that experience?
3. Have you ever discriminated against someone because of their race or color? What did you learn in this experience?

4. Write a story about how you live between two separate cultures (e.g., male and female, religious and secular, rich and poor, etc.). Show how you are able to exist between these two worlds.

5. Have you ever been a silent or active supporter of a bully, or of someone who uses the support of others to promote and gain acceptance of their own agenda? Why did you support them?

6. Have you ever supported a spouse or family member or friend, whose actions you disapproved of, because you were afraid to confront them?

7. Have you ever been a silent supporter of bullying in your community, either at the social or political levels? Describe your experience in this regard.

Afterword

Bullying is a huge problem, and not just in our schools. It exists everywhere: in our workplaces and in our homes, in our clubs and in our professional organizations, in our most intimate relationships and in our international politics. Schoolyard bullying is a microcosm of the world at large. The question is: are we content to be bystanders, or can we find the moral courage, like Alexander, to do something about it?

As a very first step, we need to recognize that bullying exists and that it is poisonous to our society. It is often a cause of addictions (food, smoking, drinking, drugs, work), physical and mental illness, suicide, family breakdown, and crime.

The big work ahead is to change societal attitudes. Most adults tell me that "bullying is a little kid's problem"; that it occurs during the early school years and is a natural behavior that has to be curbed, but that kids outgrow it. Many adults also say that if a kid is being picked on, there must be a good reason – the child is too timid, has a poor self-image, is weak in some way. Unfortunately, some of these opinions are held by parents, teachers, and principals who could make a huge difference in the problem. I myself have been bullied for bringing up the topic, for doing a bully show in my own school, where teachers told me, "It's not an issue. Get over it!"

However, adults who have a child who has been bullied, or who still remember the pain of their own experiences of bullying – these adults know first-hand the devastation that can result from bullying that isn't addressed, and they tend to have a different attitude.

It is important to remember that just because we don't always hear about bullying doesn't mean it isn't happening right under our noses. Bullies thrive in secrecy, so teachers, parents, and principals need to be vigilant and open to the reality of school life.

Another problem is that many parents protect their children from any responsibility for bullying and become aggressive themselves if their child is accused of bullying. Many principals have gotten more than an earful when they have called a bully's home to report a serious incident: "How dare you 'pick on' my child in this way!" "What kind of a school are you running that you can accuse my child like this?!"

Addressing the problem of bullying at any level takes courage and confidence in the fact that you know what you are talking about.

Bullying is an ongoing activity that doesn't stop at the end of school. The scars of bullying (for victim and bully alike) remain for life and have squelched the imagination and abilities of countless people. Yet often, even if only one person opens their eyes and starts talking about bullying – in their home, workplace, or community – it is enough to begin a process that leads to positive and lasting change. So let's speak up and stop supporting the bullies in our midst by our silence.

Suggested Reading

Beane, Allan L. *The Bully-Free Classroom: Over 100 Tips and Strategies for Teachers K–8*. Minneapolis: Free Spirit Publishing, 1999.

Chodzinski, Raymond. *Bullying: A Crisis in Our Schools and Communities*. Welland, ON: Soleil Publishing Inc., 2005.

Colorosa, Barabara. *The Bully, the Bullied, and the Bystander: From Pre-School to High School*. New York: HarperResource, 2005.

Hoover, John H. *Bullying Prevention Handbook: A Guide for Principals, Teachers, and Counselors*. Bloomington, IN: National Education Service, 1997.

Olweus, Dan. *Bullying at School: What We Know and What We Can Do*. Malden, MA: Blackwell Publishing, 1993.

Pepler, D. J., W. M. Craig, and S. Hymel. A National Strategy on Bullying: Making Canada Safer for Children and Youth. Ottawa: National Crime Prevention Center, Department of Justice, 2002.

Rigby, Ken. *Stop the Bullying: A Handbook for Teachers*. Markham, ON: Pembroke Publishing Ltd., 2002.

Suggested Website

www. bullyonline.org

About Helen Carmichael Porter

For over 20 years, Helen Carmichael Porter, a former high school teacher, has been one of Canada's best-known professional storytellers. She has told her stories onstage (National Arts Centre, St. Lawrence Centre, Factory Theatre, Blyth Festival, Bronfman Theatre), in art galleries (Art Gallery of Ontario, Royal Ontario Museum), and on CBC radio, TV, and in film. She has also toured countless schools across the country with her innovative shows of myths, folk, fairy, and personal tales. She leads popular writing workshops at the University of Toronto and across the country. Her shows of Bully stories have toured for over eight years and were created from interviews with over 300 people of all ages.